C000198749

CAERNARVON

AND THE LINES FROM

AFONWEN AND LLANBERIS

Caernarvon Harbour. March 1958. A Derby 'Lightweight' 2-car DMU bound for Pwllheli emerges from Caernarvon Tunnel under Castle Square, and passes the site of the former Carnarvon No.3 signal box. The right hand line was the Llanberis branch. The line on St.Helen's Road was still very much in use, but wagons were not now seen directly underneath the castle. Until 1962 the quayside lines were retained, designated as of strategic importance. From the mid 1930's wagons for the siding were propelled down to the quayside by trip working from the station goods yard. Engines were not permitted to work beyond the gate, so wagons were propelled through and, until 1953, moved by horse when a modified agricultural tractor fitted with a buffing plate was provided. This is the probable limit of the Welsh Highland Railway's new terminus in the town. Sadly the narrow gauge trains will not be able to thunder up the 1 in 40 gradient as the standard gauge trains did formerly. The tunnel is to be used as a by-pass road.

W.G. Rear.

BILL REAR

Copyright © Foxline Publishing & Bill Rear
ISBN 1 870119 42 8
All rights reserved
Designed and Edited by Gregory K. Fox
Typeset by Bill Rear, Johnstown, Wrexham
Printed by the Amadeus Press, Huddersfield

Published by Foxline Publishing
32 Urwick Road, Romiley, Stockport SK6 3JS

Contents:

Caernarvon. June 1934. A magnificent view of the town and surrounding countryside. In the foreground [1] the Afonwen and Llanberis lines follow the contour of the river. The two single lines levelled off briefly by the gasworks [2]. The small jetty [3] was former Welsh Highland Railway property, site of their original proposed Caernarvon terminus. This area was developed during World War II for industrial use. As the lines pass under the footbridge [4] the buildings between the lines and the harbour were part of the De Winton works, and will probably be the site of the new Welsh Highland Railway station. At one time there was a junction and signal box (Carnarvon No.3) immediately beyond the footbridge and under the retaining wall but these were removed to the passenger station about the turn of the century. The lines pass under Castle Square [5] through Caernarvon Tunnel and climb from sea level behind Bangor Street to reach the passenger station [6] which is close to Christ Church [7] identified by the spire. Behind the Church and the Crosville Bus Depot can be seen the Goods Shed, beyond that is the Victoria Dock, now undergoing development. The Coal Sidings [8] were at a lower level to the main yard and passenger station. Also visible is the Locomotive Shed [9] that was closed in 1931 but still used for stabling purposes until 1938. The line to Bangor follows the Menai Straits. The castle dominates the view but the old walled town with its network of narrow streets occupied a very small area. Just visible on the right hand edge [10] can be seen markings that were the site of the Roman garrison of Segontium. Across the water, on Anglesey, is the hamlet of Foel, with its small jetty from where 20-passenger open motor boats worked a regular ferry service across the straits to the mainland until the late 1950's. On the middle left edge of the picture can be seen the Aber swing bridge which was replaced in the 1970's with a swing pedestrian footbridge. *Airviews No.45189.*

Acknowledgements

Once again I must express thanks to those people whose contribution to this work in one way or another has been invaluable. My many friends in British Rail at Chester, but in particular, Bob Dennis. Assistance was given by Clwyd Record Office and Gwynedd Archives, and by Brian Bigwood, of Gwynedd County Council and the Chartered Institute of Transport; Arfon Haines Davies of broadcasting fame for encouragement and support. Greg Fox, for work on track plans and drawings, Hywel Gwynfryn of BBC Radio Wales for interest shown and advice given. Norman Jones, for on-going support and collaboration. To Sophia Pari Jones of Penygroes, for encouragement and support in tracking down photographs. John Kimberley for advice and support. Norman Lee of The L.N.W.R. Society for photographic assistance. The LNWR Society have been most fortunate in acquiring the majority of the negatives taken by the late J.M. Dunn. Bill Lynn of the North British Railway Study Group for collaboration. Jack and Mary Marrow of Maenan, Llanrwst, good friends, for on-going support. Gordon Rushton, late of the Ffestiniog Railway, for collaboration and encouragement. Richard Strange - Steam Archive Services for on-going assistance and collaboration particularly with engine transfers, Gareth Haulfryn Williams for encouragement and advice, and Gwenlli and Rol Williams of Waunfawr, for interest and support.

Especial thanks must be extended to Norman Kneale of Menai Bridge for his superb photographs so freely given. Also D.H. Ballantyne, Chris. and Mike Bentley, the late W.A. Camwell, the late H.C. Casserley, Brian Cowlishaw, the late J.M. Dunn, T.J. Edgington, A. Wyn Hobson, the late J.W.T. House, E.M. Johnson, Lens of Sutton, M.J. Mensing, J.H. Moss, the late G.H. Platt, H.B. Priestley, D. Rutherford, Tom Sherratt, R.H. Short, Neville Stead, Stuart Taylor, and D. Thompson.

The Ordnance Survey kindly gave permission to use extracts from their early edition large scale maps.

Thanks are extended to Jacqueline and Greg Fox, my publishers, whose continued faith in my ability to assemble this work is most gratifying. However this work could not and would not have been completed without the encouragement and ongoing support of my wife Norma, who has put up with the upheaval to her routine on what seems to be a permanent basis, and has given me the freedom to pursue research without complaining. Finally this work is dedicated to our grandson Daniel, aged three and now beginning to comprehend just how important railways are to me, and developing a personal interest which I trust will remain with him throughout his life.   Bill Rear
                                                                                                                                                    May 1996.

Caernarvon. July 1967. B.R. Standard Class 4MT 4-6-0 No. **75009** of 6G Shed (Llandudno Junction) stands alongside No.2. signal box after closure of the Afonwen and Llanberis lines, awaiting departure time to proceed along the Llanberis branch with a demolition train working. The signal box has a neglected air about it, the paintwork flaking and the windows dirty - a far cry from the spotless condition of but a few years earlier. The Afonwen starter stands devoid of coloured lenses in the arm whilst discarded materials litter the foot of the steps to the cabin. Behind the locomotive stands the wooden goods shed, now empty, out of use and devoid of life, shortly to be demolished.   *E.N. Kneale.*

Caernarvon. August 1964. B.R. Standard Class 4 4-6-0 No.**75027** stands at the Up & Down platform working the 7.45am SO Pwllheli to Manchester Exchange. The Down working left Bangor for Pwllheli at 5.30am. During the week, this working ran under Class 2 lamps and in the same running times but terminated at Bangor, and was hauled by one of 6H shed's numerous 2-6-4T. On Saturdays however the normal coaching set of four vehicles was strengthened to eight, the train ran under class 1 headlamps and suitable motive power on hand at Chester was requisitioned. Bangor men were in charge along the branch, and they worked the train through to Llandudno Junction where they were relieved by Warrington men. The train stopped all stations to Bangor, then ran non-stop to Llandudno Junction. Next stop was Prestatyn then non stop on the fast lines to Warrington, through Earlestown to Manchester where it was due at 12/58pm. Frequently it was halted outside Chester due to all roads through the station occupied. *E.N. Kneale.*

Historical.

The first railway to reach Caernarvon was the Bangor & Carnarvon Railway, incorporated on 20th May 1851, and was initially a single track line constructed from Menai Bridge to Port Dinorwic quay. At Menai Bridge, a junction was made with the Chester & Holyhead Railway, who leased the line from the Bangor & Carnarvon, although the C. & H. was worked by the L.& N.W.R., whilst Up trains could work directly onto the C. & H. Up line, Down trains for Caernarvon had no direct access and were required to draw past the station and set back into the branch platform before continuing to Caernarvon. Following an accident in 1865, the junction was altered to provide a direct double junction and an additional platform was provided on the Branch, on the Down side. Access to all platforms from the main building, which was located on the Main Line Up side, was by subway and connecting staircases.

Freight traffic commenced from Bangor to Port Dinorwic on 1st March 1852 with passenger traffic commencing nine days later. The remaining section to Caernarvon was also completed as a single line from Port Siding, about a mile north of Port Dinorwic, with Caernarvon station opening on 1st July 1852. Additional stations were opened at Griffiths Crossing in 1854 and Treborth the following year.

South of Caernarvon, the first railway into the town was The Nantlle Railway, a 3ft 6ins gauge horse drawn tramway which had opened in 1828, carrying minerals from the Nantlle valley to the quayside at Caernarvon.

The Carnarvonshire Railway was incorporated by an Act of 29th July 1862 with powers to construct a line from the Bangor & Carnarvon Railway to Portmadoc. In the event, only the section of line from Afonwen to Penygroes was built. The Cambrian Railway built the section from Afonwen to Portmadoc by agreement with the C.R. The Carnarvonshire Railway section from Penygroes to Caernarvon was abandoned when the Nantlle Railway was absorbed into the Carnarvonshire concern. Thomas Savin the contractor modified the Nantlle Railway trackbed and re-aligned and modified the line to ease curves and gradients. Progress was sufficiently advanced by February 1866 when an engine ran between Afonwen and Penygroes. The temporary northern terminus of the line was at Pant, about one and a half miles south of Caernarvon. The line was formally inspected in October 1866 but due to certain works being incomplete, official consent to open the line was withheld, eventually opening on 2nd September 1867. Stations were provided at Pwllheli Road, later renamed Llanwnda, Groeslon, Penygroes and Brynkir. A station was opened at Chwilog in 1868 and the following year, stations were authorised for Pant Glâs and Llangybi. A station was opened at Ynys in 1872. Ownership of the Carnarvonshire Railway was transferred to the LNWR in March 1869. Various proposals were made to link Llanberis with the main line in the 1860's, two at Caernarvon and the third at Bangor. Royal Assent was received by the Carnarvon & Llanberis Railway, for their proposals for the line to Caernarvon, and the ceremonial cutting of the first sod took place at Llanberis on 15th September 1864. The independent company encountered financial difficulties by 1866 and the line eventually came under the control of the L.& N.W.R., who completed construction. The branch was inspected in June 1869 and opened on 1st July. The independent concern became vested in the LNWR in July 1870. The first terminus at Caernarvon was a temporary structure, located south of the castle and near the quay, known as 'Morfa'.

So it was that there were three lines terminating at different stations in the town. Proposals were made and authorised on 5th July 1865 to link the three lines, by the Carnarvon & Llanberis, and Carnarvonshire Railway under a proposal entitled 'The Carnarvon Town Line'. The Carnarvonshire line was extended from its Pant terminus to meet the Carnarvon & Llanberis line, the two lines running parallel along the harbour before burrowing under Castle Square in Carnarvon Tunnel (163 yards), climbing behind Pool Street and Bangor Street to meet the LNWR line at an end on junction. The Carnarvon Town Line opened for freight traffic on 5th July 1870. The following month orders were given to remove Morfa station, and also the station building, goods shed and turntable at Pant. Through trains between the C. & L., and Carnarvonshire lines to Bangor were not permitted until January 1871. In that year, the Bangor & Carnarvon Railway were authorised to double the line to Menai Bridge. A second single line tunnel was bored parallel to the first line south of Treborth, known as Vaynol Tunnel.

In addition to the successful schemes mentioned, there were several standard and broad gauge proposals which failed to come to fruition but are worthy of mention. Plans were drawn up in 1852 for a Carnarvon & Portmadoc Railway, which failed to develop. The Carnarvonshire Railway originally proposed to construct a line from Caernarvon to Portmadoc, making an end-on connection with the Bangor & Carnarvon Railway via Penygroes. This was modified with the Cambrian Railways constructing and operating the section between Portmadoc and Afonwen, and the Carnarvonshire Railway's absorbing the Nantlle Tramway, and abandoning their own scheme from Penygroes to Caernarvon.

A proposed scheme was made in the 1830's to construct a line along the North Wales Coast to Porthdinllaen, which did not mature. In 1844 the 'Porthdynllaen, Carnarvon & Bangor Railway' was proposed, entitled 'North Wales Railway', the route following the coastline on the seaward side of Yr Eifl, the intention being to develop Irish traffic using Porthdinllaen as the main port for Ireland. The North Wales Railway received Royal Assent on 21st July 1845 but irregularities in its affairs destroyed the line's credibility, and, unable to muster support from the Chester & Holyhead Railway, which had initially supported the N.W.R., the latter scheme folded.

Another proposal was mooted by the Worcester & Porth Dynllaen Railway a broad gauge scheme backed by the Great Western Railway, and surveyed by Brunel. This came to nothing, as did a proposed

scheme for a standard gauge line entitled 'Great Welsh Junction Railway, with lines from Bangor and Porth Dinllaen joining to continue to Harlech and Dolgellau and then on to Shrewsbury, Hereford and Monmouth, and through South Wales, terminating at Pembroke.

An 1864 scheme was proposed to link Caernarvon with Llanberis which followed the Carnarvon & Bangor line as far as Griffiths Crossing before swinging east and climbing inland, and crossing the formation of the C. & L.R. line between Pontrug and Pontrhythallt, and following the same formation from Cwm y Glo. The 1864 proposal would have terminated about a quarter of a mile beyond the terminus as built, and opposite the Snowdon Mountain Railway terminus. The same year saw proposals for a 'Bangor & Llanberis Direct Railway'. The schemes were modified twice, but failed to materialise.

In 1865, the Carnarvon & Llanberis Railway proposed a new line from Pontrug through Waenfawr and Betws Garmon to Rhyd Ddu, the junction connection at Pontrug facing Llanberis. The line then crossed the plain between the Llanberis and Gwyrfai valleys and picked up the same formation east of Tryfan Junction taken by the North Wales Narrow Gauge Railway line to South Snowdon. There was some deviation between Waenfawr and Betws Garmon, largely to tap the Treflan Quarries, but at the mouth of Llyn Cwellyn, the line would have taken the west bank, whereas the NWNG line kept to the eastern side of the lake. At Rhyd Ddu, the line would have swung south to a point near Llyn y Gader, and served the slate quarries and mineral mines at the head of the Nantlle valley.

1865 also saw two proposed lines rejected; the Carnarvon, Beddgelert & Portmadoc, and the Carnarvon, Penygroes & Pwllheli Direct Lines. The former was to have connected with the B. & C. at Caernarvon, then via the Nantlle Tramway to Bontnewydd, Betws Garmon & Beddgelert, and then follow the course of Afon Glaslyn to Portmadoc. The second proposed line would also have used the Nantlle Tramway as far as Penygroes, then would have swung west to join the proposed North Wales line and south to Pwllheli.

Several other schemes were proposed in the nineteenth century, and the reader is invited to read Peter Baughan's Book '*A Regional History of North & Mid Wales*', as it is felt that the details of these schemes are outside the scope of this work.

On the narrow gauge front, apart from the Nantlle Tramway already mentioned, which was constructed to 3ft 6ins gauge, several other lines were proposed and some built, which influenced the standard gauge lines which are the subject of this work.

At Dinas, on the Caernarvon to Afonwen line, three miles south of Caernarvon, the North Wales Narrow Gauge Railway, (Powers granted by Act 35/6 Vic.Cap.175 of 6th August 1872), constructed to a nominal 2ft gauge line to Rhostryfan and Bryngwyn, where inclined tracks from quarries connected with the NWNGR line. A branch from Tryfan Junction through Waenfawr and Betws Garmon to Rhyd Ddu (South Snowdon), was authorised at the same time, although the 'branch' became the main line from quite early on, whilst the Bryngwyn line status reverted to a branch line. Traffic was exceptionally heavy during

the latter part of the 19th century, but tailed off as alternatives to slate were developed. Full details of the history of the North Wales Narrow Gauge Railway, and its successor, the Welsh Highland Railway, can be found in J.I.C. Boyd's definitive two volume history '*Narrow Gauge Railways in South Caernarvonshire, Vols I & II*' published by Oakwood Press.

The Dinorwic Quarries owners, the Assheton Smiths, built a seven mile narrow gauge (1ft 10¾ins) tramroad linking the quarry above Deiniolen, with Port Dinorwic on the Menai Straits about 1824. This line was worked with inclined planes, and horse power on the main line. However, this working was less than satisfactory, and a new line was built to 4ft 0½ins gauge linking the lower level of the quarry, on the shore of Llyn Padarn, via Brynrefail, Pontrhythallt and Bethel, to Penscoins, above Port Dinorwic village. The quarry galleries were connected with narrow gauge tracks, and wagons were raised and lowered from the galleries to the ground level by inclined planes. The narrow gauge wagons were then loaded onto carrier wagons - 4 to each wagon - and transported along the 4ft 0½ins line to Penscoins, where the narrow gauge wagons were offloaded and run down the balanced incline to the harbour, where they were stacked, and transhipped away by steamer or by the standard gauge line from Port Siding. Details of this line can be found in several books, including J.I.C. Boyd's work '*Narrow Gauge Railways in North Caernarvonshire, Vol.3.*', published by Oakwood Press.

In June 1869, the Carnarvon & Llanberis Railway was inspected and

Afonwen. 1960. All is perhaps not what it seems. Stanier Class 4MT 2-6-4T No.**42601** of Bangor (6H) Shed stands in the Up Passenger Loop platform, sporting headcode **C311**, which was the 8.05am Saturdays Only Manchester Exchange to Penychain, due Afonwen at 12/14pm. Alongside it is BR Standard Class 4 4-6-0 No.**75026** of Machynlleth shed, heading for Barmouth and beyond and carrying Class A lamps. However there was no Western Region Class A working due in Afonwen at this time. The 2-6-4T is carrying Class B lamps, which was incorrect for the working, and if the Manchester train was being worked back as empty stock, it would have carried Class C lamps. The angle of the sun is about right for mid-day, so what was going on. Was the Western Region train the 11.30am SO Pwllheli to Wrexham running very late? Doubtful. It might have been an extra train, but carries no reporting number. Was it, perhaps, the 12/45pm from Pwllheli to Birkenhead, up-graded to Class A working for the trip? Was 42601 in fact not working the C311 but in fact working the 11.23am from Bangor. Was the Bangor fireman dashing back to the loco having slaked his thirst or was he merely hurrying to put the injector on? We will never know   *Bill Rear collection.*

was opened between Morfa (Caernarvon) and Llanberis on 1st July. The LNWR worked the line from the start, and the inaugural service consisted of five trains daily. The Carnarvonshire and Carnarvon & Llanberis lines were not physically connected with the LNWR, and it was necessary to work the stock for the Llanberis line over the Cambrian and Carnarvonshire lines.

The connecting link, known as the 'Carnarvon Town Line' involved tunneling under Castle Square, the tunnel itself bridging Afon Cadnant, which flooded whenever the river was in spate. Near to the southern entrance of Caernarvon Tunnel, a scissors crossover was located, controlled from Carnarvon No.3 Signal Box. This track arrangement survived until 1894 when Caernarvon station was rebuilt. The cross-over was removed to the south end of the station, movements controlled from No.2 signal box. From the harbour, at sea level, it climbed at a gradient of 1 in 40 behind Pool Street and Bangor Street and made an end on connection with the Bangor & Carnarvon line. This line opened to freight traffic on 5th July 1870.

The LNWR was under obligation to build a station below Segontium Terrace, south of Caernarvon Tunnel, which would have had an island platform and offices at street level, but space was very tight, and in return for a contribution towards the construction of Bridge Street, the Corporation waived its claim to the station. The location would have been central to the town, and in later years, when buses loaded and discharged to and from all outlying villages and towns in the area, would have been very convenient. Four times in later years, the proposal to build a station at this point was resurrected and considered,

the last occasion, in 1989, being part of a project to rebuild the line between Menai Bridge and Caernarfon for passenger traffic. In 1990 another suggestion was to reconstruct the line between Menai Bridge and Nantlle for freight traffic; domestic refuse from London would have been carried and tipped into the Dorothea Quarry. A return traffic of slate waste from the quarry to Caernarfon harbour where it would be loaded into ships and carried to Germany was envisaged. Provision was made in both proposals for passenger trains to run between Bangor and Caernarfon, the passenger station platform was once more proposed to be sited under Segontium Terrace.

On a positive note, part of the Carnarvonshire Railway will nevertheless rise phoenix-like, to become the trackbed for the Welsh Highland Railway (under Festiniog Railway control), thus achieving the ultimate aim and ambitions of the old NWNGR to reach Caernarvon. At the time of writing (February 1996), planning permission has been granted for the Caernarfon to Dinas section, and the Light Railway Order drafting is in its final stages. Construction of this line should commence in 1996.

With the physical connection between the three lines made, orders were given for Morfa station, and Pant station, goods shed and turntable to be removed in August 1870, although through running for passenger traffic was not authorised until January 1871.

The late J.M. Dunn had copies of confidential proposals which the author saw briefly in 1951 that, when the determining of the Regional Boundaries was being considered in 1948, two proposals were under consideration which would have affected the lines through Caernar-

Pant Glas. August 1952. Ivatt Class 2MT 2-6-2T No.**41239** pilots Stanier Class 3 2-6-2T No.**40083**, both of 6G Llandudno Junction shed as they coast down the gradient from the summit of the line and seen here approaching Pant Glas level crossing and station. The pairing of these two locomotives was not unusual for the line. This working was the 1/20pm SO. from Llandudno Junction, Reporting Number 467, hence the two Junction tank engines on this working, and which was the normal practice for this train. Locomotives and stock then worked back to Llandudno Junction as ECS. Both footplate crews were Bangor men, and it was one of the extra Saturday turns that were handled by passed firemen working as drivers. At one time a short siding existed on the Down side of the track at this point, but this was lifted just after the Second World War.
                                                                                                                                                    W.G. Rear.

von. The first was a proposal to transfer all lines in North Wales from the London Midland Region (Western Division), to the Western Region. The notes attached to the minute from the District Engineer at Bangor indicated that the necessary costs incurred to provide adequate clearances at platforms and other structures would have been prohibitive, and the proposal was recommended for rejection. The second proposal, dated December 1948 suggested that the line from Afonwen to Caernarvon be transferred to the Western Region, with the latter station remaining in L.M.Region control. The line would come under Oswestry Area control, and Portmadoc, Pwllheli and Penmaenpool men would be required to learn the road. The modifications necessary to platforms, lines etc for re-alignment to accommodate the wider loading gauge was not considered unreasonable. Mr Dunn, however, on behalf of his staff, objected to the proposal, and it was not pursued further. Unfortunately, these papers were not included in those personal notes and effects now in the author's possession. It is interesting to speculate how the lines would have fared under Western Region control had the proposal come about.

Train Working

The earliest train services were worked by the LNWR for the C&HR who had agreed to work the B. & C. from Port Dinorwic, with the first

recorded slate train running on 10th March 1852. Passenger trains to and from Caernarvon commenced on 1st July the same year, the line finally opened to freight traffic from 10th August. By 1853 there were four trains each way on weekdays and two on Sundays. Mails were carried from 1st October 1854. By 1860 these had increased to six weekday trains and three on Sundays each way. The Working Time Tables for August 1862 show a service of seven passenger trains each way, Monday to Saturday, mostly worked by Caernarvon engines and men, and a service of three trains each way on Sundays.

South of Caernarvon, the Nantlle Tramway was operating four passenger trains each way daily in 1852, using eight horses, and a further four horses worked a Portmadoc to Penygroes omnibus. By February 1866 an engine was reported running between Afonwen and Penygroes, whilst on 6th September of the same year an excursion train was run from Portmadoc to Caernarvon whilst still awaiting Board of Trade Inspection. Alas, there was a derailment at Brynkir, in which six people were killed. The Coroner found the Railway Company not to blame. The line was formally inspected the following month. The line finally opened to traffic on 2nd September 1867 between Pant (Caernarvon) and Afonwen and until 10th October of the same year, extended their services over Cambrian Railway metals to Criccieth, Portmadoc and Penrhyndeudraeth. Initially Cambrian Rail-

Penygroes. February 1955. From 1946 Bangor locomotive stock increasingly included locomotives of the 2-6-4 wheel arrangement, which were ideally suited to the steeply graded Afonwen line. Initially the allocation consisted of Stanier and Fairburn versions of this wheel arrangement, but in 1954 four Fairburn tanks were sent to Gourock in exchange for four of the older Fowler tanks, Nos.42415-8. Despite the enclosed cabs they were popular engines, regarded as slightly more powerful than their younger cousins. Here No.**42416** blows off furiously whilst standing at the Down platform with the 12/20pm from Bangor. The signalman walks up to the loco carrying the staff for the section to Brynkir. A couple of passengers wait on the Up side. Notice the tidy appearance of the platform, with the flower beds and trellis work prepared for the floral display that was a hallmark of this station during the summer months, and for which they won 'best garden' prizes with regularity. The 'hawkseye' station sign persisted until the line closed, although new totems had been supplied in 1950. The footbridge has now gone, but the road overbridge beyond it still stands. Its girders still carry the wording 'De Winton' cast into the sides, a relic from the days when the Carnarvon foundry supplied materials to the Carnarvonshire Railway who built the line.   *W.A. Camwell.*

ways engines were used until the Carnarvonshire accepted delivery of its own engines, built by Sharp, Stewart & Co in May 1868, a second locomotive being delivered in December. From 25th July 1867, reciprocal running powers were agreed with the Cambrian between Caernarvon, Portmadoc and Pwllheli, which were rescinded when the LNWR took over control.

Traffic continued to grow, and in 1871, powers to double the line between Menai Bridge and Caernarvon, including excavating a second bore at Vaynol tunnel, were authorised.

In 1894, an Up platform, footbridge and additional sidings were installed at Caernarvon.

Temporary platforms were erected in the yard for special trains on 13th July 1911 for the Investiture of the Prince of Wales. On that day, Cambrian Railways locomotives and men from Portmadoc shed worked services over the former Carnarvonshire lines.

The GWR Running Powers Book shows that running powers were available to the LMS over the Cambrian Coast and Corwen to Barmouth Junction lines, and the GWR were afforded similar facilities over the Denbigh, Ruthin & Corwen, Vale of Clwyd and Afonwen lines, with the proviso that the 'visiting' enginemen were piloted over the home company's tracks. These facilities continued until the branch lines were severed, but rarely invoked.

It is believed that there was some through locomotive working before the First World War, but details are not known. First positive references are abstracted from the Cambrian Railways Working Time Book for May 5th 1919 until further notice. These show an Empty Stock train departing Afonwen for Portmadoc daily at 12.05pm labelled "*LNWR Engine and Train*", working back to Afonwen as the 12.38pm Passenger. Another LNWR working to Portmadoc departed Afonwen at 5.18pm and returned with an Empty Stock working from there at 5.55pm. An LNWR Engine and train worked to Pwllheli at 2.55pm, returning from there to Afonwen at 3.35pm. There is no mention of through working in the equivalent LNWR Working Time Tables for the same period. Likewise, in post grouping days, there is no indication in LMS Working Time Tables of through working to Portmadoc or Pwllheli until 1938, when two Sunday workings by LMS locos and trains to Pwllheli are shown. However the GWR Service Time Table Section 14, for September 11th 1933 to July 15th 1934 shows an LMS Auto train departing Afonwen for Pwllheli at 11.23am, SX, returning with the 12.10pm to Afonwen. The GWR Service Time Table Section 14 for July 8th to September 29th 1935 shows three LMS passenger workings departing Afonwen for Pwllheli on Sundays Only, at 12.15pm, 3.15pm and 7.50pm, returning at 12.50pm, 5.10pm and 8.20pm respectively. The GWR Section 16 Service Time Table for July 4th to September 25th 1938 also shows the two LMS workings, departing Bangor at 10.20am and 2.00pm, Caernarvon 10.40am and 2.20pm and Afonwen at 11.39am and 3.29pm, returning from Pwllheli at 12.15pm and 5.00pm, Afonwen at 12.35pm and 5.25pm, Caernarvon at 1.28pm and 6.18pm arriving at Bangor at 1.44pm and 6.33pm respectively. The LMS Working Time Table for 2nd July to 24th September 1939 showed the workings in the same timings.

Services over the Afonwen line weekdays was fairly static, and services between the wars declined with the recession following the General Strike. The winter period, from late September to April saw on average eleven trains each way over the line on weekdays, with another eleven trains between Bangor and Caernarvon, some of these

extending to Llanberis. On Saturdays, this extended to sixteen trains to Afonwen and nine between Bangor and Caernarvon or Llanberis. On Sundays there were six trains each way between Bangor and Caernarvon. As the country climbed out of the recession, the services increased, and the period from 2nd July to 24th September 1939 saw eleven trains daily, SX between Bangor & Afonwen, with eighteen on Saturdays and two on Sundays, and eleven between Bangor and Caernarvon or Llanberis weekdays and nine on Sundays between Bangor and Caernarvon, one of which was extended to Llanberis.

Emergency services were introduced on 11th September 1939 with the outbreak of World War II, and three trains each way between Bangor and Afonwen sufficed, with two additional trains between Bangor and Caernarvon SX, five on Saturdays and two on Sundays. This improved by 1st January 1940 when six trains ran to Afonwen and return weekdays, and eight on Saturdays. In addition, three trains ran to Caernarvon SX, and four on Saturdays. There were no Sunday trains.

The Passenger Working Time Table from October 4th 1943 to April 30th 1944 showed the introduction of new workings. An unadvertised special ran daily, Tuesdays to Saturdays departing Afonwen at 6.15am, Reporting Number 678 conveying Naval Personnel to Crewe from *HMS Glendower*, based at Penychain, which became Butlins Camp after the war. During the week, naval staff travelled back by ordinary passenger trains, but on Sunday night/Monday mornings, a Naval Special ran from Crewe, departing at 4.30am, Reporting Number 679, and changed locomotives at Bangor, departing there at 6.55am, reaching Afonwen at 8.32am. This working continued until, and was shown in the Passenger Working Time Table for October 1st 1945, although the timings were adjusted slightly. The Reporting Numbers remained the same for both Up and Down journeys. Also included in the passenger workings was Monday to Saturday Milk Special Workings, designated 'Parcels' traffic, that ran every evening from Chwilog to Broad Green. The duty was worked throughout by Bangor men, who lodged overnight at Edge Hill. The return working was with ordinary passenger train working to Bangor, where the crew changed and took the milk empties forward to Afonwen, and after running around the stock, worked it to Chwilog, where the vans were shunted into the siding and the loco returned L.E. to Bangor. At one time, five six-wheeled vans comprised the train to Bangor, and a similar load was attached there, from Gaerwen, and worked forward. By October 1945 the Empty Stock timings had altered but the Up working remained the same. The working times had altered by May 1948 and the train departed Chwilog at 7.40pm. Twelve months later, the traffic had been lost to road tankers.

On Wednesday 29th January 1947, loading tests between Llandudno Junction, Bangor and Afonwen were undertaken with Class 4MTT STD 2-6-4T No.**2260**, driver W. Graham, with a load of 10 corridor coaches, 302 tons, under the supervision of Footplate Inspector G.L. Stephenson, to assess the capability of this class of locomotive when handling ten coach trains unassisted and to determine the motive power needs for working similar capacity trains to Butlin's Holiday Camp at Penychain the following summer. The tests indicated that whilst the loco and driver worked to the schedule, there was an insufficient margin of safety to consider single locomotive working. The recommendation was to reduce the load to 8 coaches, 240 tons, or pilot ten coach trains. Since line occupancy would be fully stretched, it was necessary to work ten coach trains, and therefore

Near Penygroes. 16th July 1960. BR Standard Class 4MT 4-6-0 No.**75054** of Rhyl Shed (6K) heads south with *The Welsh Chieftain* Land Cruise working from Rhyl to Barmouth via Caernarvon, returning via Bala and Corwen. The train ran Mondays to Fridays in the season, from the last week in June until the first week in September. Departure from Rhyl was at 9.25am and progress was leisurely to say the least, so that passengers could appreciate the scenery. A counterpart working was the Cambrian Radio Land Cruise, that worked the circuit in the opposite direction. One of the coach sets included the former 'Devon Belle' Observation Coach, and the vehicle can just be seen at the end of the formation. Rhyl men worked both trains and the extra work enabled passed firemen at the depot to chalk up driving turns which were otherwise hard to come by. After taking water at Caernarvon, the train worked without stopping to Brynkir, where it crossed with the 10.50am from Afonwen. It then continued without stopping (in theory) to Portmadoc, where it took water once more. Barmouth was reached about 12/20pm and 90 minutes were allowed for passengers to explore the town. When the line was being built, enough land was taken for double track formation, but traffic never justified the provision. The bridge is a standard Carnarvonshire Railway design, the brick facing being of local yellow brick. *R.H. Short.*

piloting of all passenger trains over 240 tons was considered necessary, a decision which had profound effects on Bangor shed workings for the next fifteen years.

From 1948 to 1963 the line experienced seasonal fluctuations. Nationalisation saw London Midland Region locomotives commenced working through to Pwllheli on a daily basis, eliminating the need for the Western Region to provide power as formerly, which had an adverse effect on Portmadoc and Pwllheli shed work. From 1948 Bangor engines and men worked to and from Portmadoc on the '*Welshman*' workings, but due to weight restrictions, Stanier Class 3 2-6-2T were the largest motive power allowed. In 1948 the Down '*Welshman*' working worked through from Bangor to Portmadoc, but this was not repeated in following years, although the morning 'Up' working remained a Bangor turn until the line closed. With the introduction of diesel multiple units from 1957, a basic winter service of eight trains each way to Afonwen of which seven worked through to Pwllheli, together with three trips between Bangor and Caernarvon and return, prevailed. The summer season saw increases in traffic during the week, and in the holiday season, Land Cruise trains worked over the line in one direction, although latterly some additional Cruise trains worked the reverse direction, with as many as four trains daily at its peak. Eleven trains ran daily, Monday to Friday, each way, with three workings to Caernarvon and one working to Llanberis. On Saturdays, however, there were seventeen workings from Bangor to

Penychain or Pwllheli and return, excluding Light Engine workings, and an additional three workings to and from Caernarvon. On peak Saturdays, every passing loop along the line was occupied, trains frequently being held up awaiting the train staff, and it was not uncommon for trains running late into Bangor being held there for nearly an hour, awaiting a change of locomotive, for most trains over the Afonwen line were double headed by tank engines of various permutations. The double track line to Caernarvon created a false sense of optimism, as the eight miles were run off in what seemed record times, usually about fifteen minutes. Most trains took water at Caernarvon, entailing drawing up to gain access to the column at the end of the Up and Down platform, and then the waiting started again. A double headed return working laboriously climbed the 1 in 40 gradient from the harbour up to No.2 signal box, and the signalman would take the staff, hurry to the box and replace it in the token machine, and amid a flurry of bells, withdraw it again, and hand it to the driver, who would toot to draw attention to the second driver, open the regulator briefly, and then coast down the 1 in 40, through Carnarvon Tunnel to the harbour, where they twin exhausts would blast forth as the climb to Dinas commenced. The gradient was almost as severe, and the three and a half miles would be unremitting slog for the firemen, with ten heavily laden corridor coaches. At Dinas the train would draw to a halt, and hand over the staff to the signalman, who would dash up to the box and insert it in the instrument, withdrawing it immediately for an Up train that was bearing down from Groeslon. The policy was to keep the home signal at danger and as the Up train passed through Llanwnda, would whistle up for the home. Entrance to the Up loop was severe, and the speed restriction was meticulously observed by all concerned. Token and Staff change-over was performed in front of the box, on the Up platform, and once the change had been effected, the signalman dashed back up the steps to the box to give 'Train Entering Section' to Caernarvon No.2 box, and clear the token back to Groeslon, before asking 'Is Line Clear...' for the Down working still standing. This was repeated at Groeslon, Penygroes, Brynkir and Llangybi, and however smartly the tokens were exchanged, however hard the drivers worked their engines and firemen, it was as much as one could do to keep to running time, never mind making up lost time. Passenger trains could not cross at Chwilog, for there was no passing loop but a passenger train could cross a locomotive or freight train provided it was safely locked in in the goods yard or the milk siding south of the level crossing. The token was exchanged for a train staff and trains were brought to a halt for the purpose at the platform, the instruments being located in the office, whilst the frame was on the platform at the Afonwen end. It was the practice to release the brakes and apply light steam to get the train moving, and then coast down to Afonwen, braking steadily all the way, for it was a certainty that the train would be held at the junction with the Pwllheli line, whilst awaiting a platform road. Eventually the arm would come 'off' and the last half mile to Afonwen would be covered in a minute or so. Most Butlin's trains were ten coaches in length, and the platforms had been extended just before the war to accommodate longer trains. Once at a halt, the fireman on the train engine would nip down onto the tracks and uncouple the stock, whilst his mate would produce a lamp with red shade for the light engine movement beyond the crossover. A quick change of lamps on both engines and a toot on the whistle, and another to acknowledge the signalman response of giving the road, and then set back, through the Down main road till the crossover was clear, change the lamps once more, and toot up the signalman. Having got the road, the train engine opened up and set back onto the stock. The pilot engine fireman then changed the headcode whilst the train engine fireman coupled up and removed his lamp, and it was then time to be 'off'. The movement was straightforward, but if the three platform faces were occupied it became necessary to run round using the Up side goods loop, and frequently a wait was necessary until the signalman could permit the move to continue. The track to Penychain was double line, and the run took only five minutes from Afonwen. The empty stock would be worked forward to Pwllheli East and stabled, or worked back to Afonwen, where it was parked for a short while, beyond the platform on the Criccieth side until the path for the return working became available. Frequently it was necessary to move the locomotives to the ashpit road, to take on water from the twin tanks on the Down side, and to clean the fire. Frequently there could be as many as four engines standing on the ashpit road, and an L.M. Region Inspector was on duty throughout the day to the sort out the apparent confusion. It was not unusual to part company with one's pilot or train engine and couple up to another locomotive for the return working up the line. Some stock stopped at Pwllheli East for the week and locos thus released worked back light engine to Bangor as quickly as possible whilst others would be utilised to pilot trains to Caernarvon, Bangor or Llandudno Junction. It was not

uncommon to see ten locomotives at Afonwen about mid-day on busy Saturdays. The regular Western Region staff were assisted by L.M. Region Traffic Inspectors, who generally kept a low profile, acknowledging that the local man knew best, and left him to it. It was not always so, though, and on occasions a 'know-all' arrived, and who proceeded to shout his mouth off displaying his superiority (and ignorance) to the multitudes, who remained disinterested in his performance. It was on such an occasion that the visiting 'brains trust' allocated a Class Five 4-6-0 as train engine, facing tender first, and piloted by another Class Five 4-6-0 with smokebox leading, and despite the protestations that the locomotive positions should be reversed, ignored all advice and despatched the train to Warrington. At Caernarvon, the pilot engine detached as per instructions, and the 6H men on the train engine proceeded alone, tender first to Bangor, where they handed over to Chester men, who worked the train (tender first) all the way to Chester. There comments were voiced to every official who dared show his face, but there was no time or facility to rectify the situation, and they worked from block post to block post, cursing volubly every inch of the way. It might have been less irritating had the weather been fine, but it was a gusty day with driving rain, and coal dust swirled around the cab to add to the discomfort. The Warrington men who relieved our heroes at Chester were equally impressed with the Inspector's abilities, and just as vocal in their praises, called his parentage into question! This was an exceptional case, but the 'brains trust' were just as likely to mess things up in other ways. One such gentleman in July 1954 was anxious about the build-up of motive power hanging around the Ashpit road one Saturday afternoon, and misreading his power requirements, despatched several 2-6-4T locomotives back to Bangor Light Engines. It so happened that an additional train comprising of four coaches had been added to the Supplementary Notice of Special Trains at short notice, and was running that day from Llandudno Junction to Penychain, and then worked back ECS to Afonwen. The train was scheduled to return coupled to an additional six coaches which were standing temporarily in the Up sidings, the whole then worked to Menai Bridge and then to Holyhead. A 2-6-4T was allocated to pilot the ECS to Menai Bridge, where they would come off the train and return LE to the shed. The 'brains trust' found to his horror that he had dismissed the pilot loco and an Ivatt Class 2MT 2-6-2T was the sole motive power available to work the ECS, and which was clearly outclassed, although the driver in question was quite willing to 'have a go'. After a flurry of telephone calls, the ECS stock was parked in the Up side sidings whilst a locomotive was despatched from Bangor to assist the 2-6-2T and a driver and fireman made their third trip of the day to Afonwen. The Inspector was never allowed to forget it and was not seen at Afonwen again!

The introduction of DMU's to the line saw their limited use at first, with only two such trains working through to Afonwen or Pwllheli. This traffic was largely in the hands of Derby 'Lightweight' units, replaced in time by Metropolitan-Cammell two car units, which handled the requirements of the line satisfactorily, with most of the services still in the hands of 2-6-4T locomotives. By the winter period of the 1959 season this had changed, when all but the second passenger train of the day was handled by diesels. The Summer season saw reversion to steam hauled trains for most workings and this pattern persisted until as late as September 1963, with only one DMU worked through to Afonwen daily whilst for the 1964 summer season, the final one for the line as it happened, repeated this pattern with only the last three trains of the day being worked by DMU's. The final months of the branch saw all the passenger services with the exception of the 5.20am from Bangor to Pwllheli and the 7.45am return working DMU worked.

The Nantlle branch passenger service had been in the care of 'motor' trains off and on from the early days of the century. The journey was short in duration, and necessitated changing at Penygroes most times. Only the first Down and Last Up trains worked from and to Caernarvon. During the First World War a Petrol Electric Railcar had been used, but the experiment was not a success, partly because the roof mounted radiator froze over in the winter, and more importantly, the single coach unit was not capable of shunting or pulling more than its own weight. It was reported as also working on the Bethesda and Llanberis lines, without success. Traffic was sufficiently poor to justify closing the line to passenger traffic from 1st January 1917 for the

duration, restored on 5th May 1919. Buses were found to be more convenient and regular passenger traffic ceased on 8th August 1932, although some excursion trains continued to run until the outbreak of World War II. Apart from occasional Private Charter trains run towards the end of the line's days, no passenger trains ran to and from Nantlle again.

The Llanberis branch passenger traffic remained fairly constant, albeit at a low level, until the General Strike when passengers were lost to buses and never regained. Various experiments were tried to encourage trade, including the use of 'motor' trains, but the half mile walk from Caernarvon station to the town centre proved an obstacle. A single road locomotive shed was built for the opening of the line, and the branch trains were worked by Llanberis men, until the shed was closed some time after July 1915, when the engine and seven men were transferred to Caernarvon. Regular passenger trains stopped running on 22nd September 1930, although regular excursion traffic continued until the outbreak of World War II. Excursions were run from Prestatyn and

Caernarvon. 1960. No.42076 of Bangor Shed working the 11.26 from Bangor (8.25am Liverpool to Pwllheli) pulls into the Up & Down platform at Caernarvon. The absence of passengers suggests that this was mid week. By this time many of the weekday passenger workings on the branch were worked by DMU but this remained a steam turn until the commencement of the winter period of operation. It will be seen that the second coach bears a carriage board indicating the through working from Liverpool. Will Rees, signalman in No.2 box, stands under the platform canopy, train staff for the single line section to Dinas in hand. The replacement buildings for the island platform were a distinct improvement on the draughty old wooden structure it replaced, but the benefits of a more compact and warmer building were offset by the lack of protection for the passengers who had to endure the stiff winds that blew off Caernarvon Bay. The powers-that-be in their wisdom decided that the footbridge covering was also in need of replacement and the expense was not justified. On fine warm days this was no hardship, but in the depths of winter, porters gained the additional job of retrieving headgear from the tracks. Only the photographer benefitted by the removal of the cover. Notice the Prince of Wales 'feathers' which decorated the gable end of the Station Master's living quarters. Just visible over the flat roof of the island platform building can be seen the brake van and locomotive off the Llanberis Goods, whilst in the distance is No.1 signal box. Today a supermarket covers the site.   *Bill Rear collection.*

Rhyl during summer months and proved very popular. An Observation Car had been attached to these seasonal workings from before 1914. There was a lot of local excursion traffic from Llanberis to Caernarvon and Llandudno, and frequently cheap day excursions were run to Liverpool and Manchester. All this traffic ceased with the outbreak of war. The day excursions from Prestatyn and Rhyl were resumed in a limited form during the summer season, from 1947 until 1962, achieving the status of a 'named' train at one stage, and shown in the publicity brochures as "*The Snowdonian*". The Observation cars were restored on this service and from 1950, the engine and car working back to Caernarvon about mid-day for servicing and crew change, running back in the middle afternoon to Llanberis in time to couple up and work back to Rhyl and Prestatyn in the evening.

Freight working on the Afonwen branch developed from the outset. Dressed slate formed the bulk of the traffic carried out of the area, balanced by coal, agricultural stock and general merchandise traffic. There was some freight interchange at Afonwen, but this was limited to whatever traffic could be directed over the line by the LNWR/LMS agents. The General Strike of 1926 hit the small slate quarry owners hard, who could not afford to lose trade, already suffering a declining market with competition from European tile manufacturers, and who, in order to survive, transferred to local road hauliers, most never to use rail services again. The loss of traffic also hit the Welsh Highland, who lost traffic from Glanrafon and Moel Tryfan Quarries, which was their main source of income, and from which they never fully recovered. This traffic was transhipped at Dinas Junction, and with the loss of traffic, one loco turn from Caernarvon, a guard and a goods clerk at Dinas were laid off. Previously, a loco had worked out from Caernarvon to Dinas, to work the mineral traffic back to Caernarvon, where it would be sorted and incorporated into the main evening mineral train to Springs Branch, and latterly cut back to Mold Junction.

Quarries in the Nantlle Valley brought their slates to Nantlle station on horse drawn narrow gauge wagons, where it was transhipped to standard gauge wagons. The density of traffic from these quarries survived despite the depression, and the train ran daily until the winter of 1956 when the working was cut back to three days a week, and alternated with the Llanberis freight, which suffered a similar fate. It lasted in this form until the line closed to all traffic on 2nd December 1963. On the Llanberis branch, goods traffic was light, and the expected slate transport never materialised, although Glynrhonwy and Hickmans Quarries used the line until the depression, when the quarries closed. There was some inward traffic, mainly coal and general stores but generally one freight trip each way sufficed until 1957 when the daily trip was cut back to alternate days. During the Second World War there was an upsurge of traffic to the Glynrhonwy Sidings, where an R.A.F. Camp was established and a Government Ordnance Factory built to assemble bombs. The components were brought in, and the finished products removed by rail, and two trains a day sufficed. After the war the quarry pit was used to dispose of surplus bombs and explosives, and the traffic flow was reversed. By 1949 this traffic had ceased, and the line survived with the limited freight carried.

Caernarvon yard was the concentration point for the branches and traffic remained heavy, until the facility was strangled under the Beeching proposals. Slate traffic from Llanberis, Nantlle and off the Welsh Highland was sorted and marshalled at Caernarvon daily, and worked to Springs Branch every evening at 10.00pm until 1926 when the work was cut back to Mold Junction. Usual motive power was an 0-8-0 G.2. locomotive, and regularly worked up to its load limit. The train was assembled in the coal yard by the freight shunt loco on duty, which worked in the lower yard from 4.00pm until departure time. The train started from the coal yard and the freight shunt loco assisted the train up the sharp gradient onto the main line before running back into the shed road where the crew disposed of the engine and signed off. The decline in mineral traffic saw the traffic diminish, but the evening departure to Mold Junction persisted until the late 1950s. A Freight Train Shunting Book for August 1936 in the possession of Gwynedd Archives gives some idea of the density of the traffic and it was common to see four or five locomotives at the same time shunting and making up various freight trains. Latterly there was a considerable amount of cattle wagon working empty to the yard from Holyhead for cleaning purposes. When this livestock traffic was terminated by B.R. in the 1960s, it had an immediate effect on the yard. During the war petroleum traffic to the town increased considerably, and large storage tanks were built on Victoria Dock. With the cessation of hostilities in 1945, this traffic survived for a few years, but was lost to costal shipping in the mid 1950s. This traffic could have kept the line open after 1969, but the maritime lobby was very strong and the railway deemed a lost cause by the local politicians, who offered no resistance to the decline and termination of rail facilities. In the years that followed the petroleum traffic was transferred from ship to road, but this was not destined to last, the depot closed and the tanks removed. Today the site is much sought after for prestige building development. Petroleum is today brought from Ellesmere Port by road tankers, adding to the chaos on the overcrowded roads.

Motive Power

Caernarvon was a station of some importance until the recession of the 1930s coupled with the development of public bus services drew traffic away from the rails and onto the roads. Until 1926, the shed worked some important long distance trains, including one Euston job throughout the year worked with Camden based Claughton class 4-6-0s, and a turn to Chester, and another summer season working to Euston, as well as regular lodging turns to Springs Branch (Wigan) with mineral traffic, returning with coal. The remainder of the work was local, some of which was shared with Bangor. After the General Strike, work was lost, never to be regained, and some men and the Euston jobs were transferred to Bangor. The Camden based Claughton 4-6-0 locomotives, numbered 6026/7/8 were regularly stabled at Caernarvon overnight. There was a minor problem with these locomotives, in that they were too long to be turned on the 42ft turntable, but the problem was overcome by detaching the tender from the loco and each was turned separately, being re-coupled afterwards. The same procedure was adopted with the tender engine Class G2 0-8-0 used on the Springs Branch job. After 1926 the locomotives were changed at Bangor. As the work retracted, the remaining duties were local in nature, and consisted mainly of trips between Bangor, Llanberis and Afonwen, although the top job worked as a lodging turn to Mold Junction with a Class 4F 0-6-0.

In LNWR days, 0-6-0 tender engines were used for both passenger and freight workings on the branch but the removal of the turntable at Afonwen put an end to the practice. Small tank engines, working in pairs then worked the branch and alternated with Bowen Cooke 4-6-2T engines which were drafted in to work over the line in the mid thirties. In the summer of 1937 two Fowler 2-6-4T engines were allocated to Bangor, and put to work on the line, with immediate success, but were transferred at the commencement of the winter duties. They were replaced by Fowler and Stanier 2-6-2T engines, but the limited water capacity and indifferent steaming performance of these engines proved a retrograde step, resulting in the loads being reduced, a situation not remedied until July 8th 1946 when Stanier 2-6-4T Nos. 2460 and 2628 were received and put to work on the line. On January 11th 1947 Fairburn 2-6-4T nos. 2258 and 2261 were received new, followed by 2260 on 13th, and 2259 on 24th of the same month, replacing four 2-6-2T engines. On 17th February 1947 Ivatt 2-6-2T No.1200 was received new from Crewe works, followed by 1201 on 3rd March. These replaced 6710 and 6926, which moved to other sheds in the district, and which reappeared at Bangor from time to time. 42460 was the first engine to receive its new British Railways number in May 1948. The following month saw another 2-6-4T arrive - 2662, standing in for 2260 which went to Crewe Works on 21st June and stayed until October, the same month that 1201 was transferred to 4D. However four new Ivatt 2-6-2T, nos 41221/2/3/4 arrived in November, together with 40087 and 143, replacing some of the older LNWR engines. The larger engines worked the Afonwen line, whilst the smaller tanks spent most of their days on the Amlwch and Bethesda branches. During this same period (1946-48) Bangor had three Stanier Class 5P5F 2-6-0 engines for its main line work, Nos. 2948/51/84, and Fowler Class 4F 0-6-0 Nos. 4305/4445 which spent their days working the Nantlle and Llanberis Goods jobs. Class 2P No.524 was used for the Chwilog Milk turn, whilst the remainder of the allocation consisted of sundry types of various vintage and pedigree. On 23rd May 1949, two more 2-6-4T were received - Nos. 42660 and 42617, whilst the

Stanier 2-6-0s were sent to Bescot on 21st June and replaced by Class 5 4-6-0 Nos. 4913, and 45417 on 23rd June and 5144 the following day. 41200 was sent to Ipswich for trials on the Aldeburgh branch on 28th June, returning back to Bangor via Crewe works on 16th November. (It returned to Ipswich on 11th May 1950 finally returning in August to Bangor, where it was to remain, apart from periodic visits to the works, until withdrawn). September saw 41221/2 transferred to Barrow and Bletchley respectively. June 1950 saw the seasonal increase with Fairburn 2-6-4T Nos 42156/7 followed by 42588 on 8th July. Two more 2-6-4T's appeared briefly in early August, No 42552 from 3D and 42599 from 9A, both returning home on 15th of the same month. 42660 departed in September leaving the winter complement of 2-6-4T at 10 locomotives for eight jobs. The following July saw 42062 from 5D and 42350 from 6A drafted in for the month, and 41287 received new. 46430 arrived from Rhyl on 21st September 1951 and staying for three weeks. Dwindling traffic saw some of the older locomotives disappear over the succeeding months, some transferred and some cut up. By July 1952 the allocation consisted largely of modern locomotives and it is worth listing the allocation in full:

Class 1PT	2-4-2T	46701, 46604 (to 6G - on loan)
Class 2MT	2-6-2T	41200, 41223, 41230, 41233, 41239, 41287,
		41324
Class 3MT	2-6-2T	40132
Class 4MT	2-6-4T	42156, 42157, 42258, 42259, 42260,
		42261, 42455, 42460, 42588, 42617, 42628.
Class 4F	0-6-0	44305, 44445.
Class 5MT	4-6-0	44913, 45144, 45417.
Class 3F	0-6-0	52119, 52162, 52230, 12269.
Class 2F	0-6-0	58375
Class 2F	0-6-2T	58903.

Afonwen. July 1963. No.80096 of Machynlleth shed (89C) pulls into the Up platform with a Class B working from Pwllheli. These Class 4 tanks saw out regular steam working over the coast line. They had replaced 82xxx Class 2-6-2T engines which in turn had replaced some 78xxx Class 2 tender engines which arrived about 1953 and had worked alongside the traditional Great Western 'Dukedogs' and those Cambrian 0-6-0's that survived into Nationalisation. Although there was some residual loyalty to the GWR, the enclosed cab and modern facilities were greatly appreciated by the former Cambrian staff who had enjoyed/endured the somewhat exposed facilities offered by the predecessors. Three escapees from Butlins head for the Refreshment Room entrance which faced the gents urinals. A strategic necessity perhaps.
Bill Rear collection.

The next major change came in April 1954 when four Fairburn 2-6-4T were exchanged for four Fowler engines of the same class. Nos.42258-62 went to Gourock in exchange for Nos.42415-8. The allocation for August 1954 was as follows:

Class 3MT	2-6-2T	40102
Class 2MT	2-6-2T	41200, 41212, 41223, 41230, 41233, 41239, 41324.
Class 4MT	2-6-4T	42156, 42157, 42178, 42415, 42416, 42417, 42418, 42444, 42455, 42460, 42588, 42617.
Class 4F	0-6-0	44305, 44445.
Class 5MT	4-6-0	44913, 45144, 45417.
Class 3F	0-6-0	52119, 52230, 52269.
Class 2F	0-6-0	58394.

In October 1956 there was a wholesale clear-out of most of the LMS design 2-6-4T locomotives, which were replaced by a batch of B.R. Standard Class 4MT 2-6-4T. The allocation was as follows:

Class 3MT	2-6-2T	40003.
Class 2MT	2-6-2T	41200, 41230, 41233, 41239.
Class 4MT	2-6-4T	42415, 42416, 80087, 80088, 80089, 80090, 80091, 80092, 80094, 80095.
Class 4F	0-6-0	44305, 44445.
Class 5MT	4-6-0	44913, 45144, 45417.
Class 3F	0-6-0	52119, 52230, 52269.
Class 0F	0-4-0T	51221. (in store).

The allocation for August 1958 was as follows:

Class 3MT	2-6-2T	40071, 40132, 40136, 40185.
Class 2MT	2-6-2T	41200, 41230, 41233, 41234, 41239.
Class 4MT	2-6-4T	42478, 42482, 42494, 42538, 42586, 42604, 42611, 42627, 80059, 80087, 80088, 80089, 80090, 80094, 80095.
Class 4F	0-6-0	44305, 44445.
Class 5MT	4-6-0	44913, 45144, 45417.
Class 3F	0-6-0T	47511, 47588.
Class 0F	0-4-0T	47006.
Class 2MT	2-6-0	78057.

With the closure of the Afonwen, Amlwch, Llanberis and Nantlle lines, work at Bangor was drastically reduced and locomotives were transferred elsewhere. The writing was on the wall for the shed, and it closed on 12th June 1965. The allocation and fate of the locomotives was as follows:

Class 2MT	2-6-2T	41200 to	6G.	Scrapped 10/65.
		41204 to	6C.	Scrapped 4/67.
		41233 to	9B.	Scrapped 12/65.
		41234 to	8G.	Scrapped 4/67.
		41241 to	10G.	Preserved K. & W.V.Rly.
Class 5MT	4-6-0	44821 to	6J.	Scrapped 12/67.
		45145 to	6J.	Scrapped 2/68.
		45223 to	6J.	Scrapped 7/67.
		45298 to	6J.	Scrapped 2/68.
		45345 to	6J.	Scrapped 9/68.
Class 2MT	2-6-0	78003 to	1A.	Scrapped 9/67.
		78032 to	1A.	Scrapped 1/66.
		78058 to	1A.	Scrapped 9/67.
		78059 to	1A.	Preserved Bluebell Railway.
Class 4MT	2-6-4T	80131		Scrapped 7/65.

Coaching

The earliest available Diagram of Carriage Working dates from 21st September 1925. The Circuit Sets involved were as follows:

Afonwen Line & Caernarvon:
184, 189, 702, 779, 782, 783, 784, 785, 829, 831

Llanberis Line: 846

Nantlle Branch: 853

Sets 184 and 189 were Inter District Sets comprising 4 vehicles -110 tons and worked between Caernarvon, Afonwen and Llandudno, alternating daily. Set 702 comprised 4 vehicles - 113 tons in was one of the Manchester and Llandudno Sets, working 7.25am Manchester Exch. to Caernarvon arriving 11.39am and worked back to Chester with the 3.35pm.SX. Sets 779-786 were Bangor District comprising 5 vehicles - 65 tons, and worked between Bangor and Afonwen, Amlwch, Llandudno Jn., and Nantlle. Set 818 (2 vehicles - 26 tons) was nominally a Llandudno Junction to Afonwen set but which worked between Bangor and Holyhead only. No.829 - 2 vehicles, 26 tons - was a strengthening set and worked one trip daily between Afonwen and Bangor. Set 831 was also 2 vehicles - 26 tons and worked between Caernarvon, Afonwen and Bangor. Set 846 was a Driving Composite and 3rd - 58 tons and worked between Carnarvon & Llanberis as a Motor Train Set. Set 853 was Nantlle Branch Motor Train Set and was a Driving third - 29 tons weight.

The six wheel stock in the circuits were replaced gradually by more modern vehicles, and the number of sets decreased accordingly. Bangor District stock was absorbed into Llandudno Junction District in the 1930s.

After World War II, many North Wales branch lines retained the local circuit stock of non corridor coaches of varying vintage, and which rarely strayed outside the district. However this was not so for the Afonwen branch, where Inter District Stock worked between Llandudno, Chester, Liverpool, Manchester, and Crewe and which made up most of the trains in steam days. Through coaching stock between Liverpool, Manchester and Euston to Portmadoc and Pwllheli was a regular feature throughout the year, perhaps more noticeable in the summer months, when activities increased. Most trains were composed of four coaches, although some workings conveyed extra vans for mail traffic. The first train of the day was made up to six vehicles with a bogie corridor brake for Portmadoc and another one for Pwllheli, which were detached at Afonwen and worked forward by the Western Region. Stock which formed 'The Welshman' was Class 'A' stock and the workings were recorded in Passenger Train Marshalling books. When the DMU's took over most of the work on the branch, the working of some of the mails was held back for the 5.00am to Pwllheli which was steam hauled until the line closed, although the bulk of the parcels traffic had been transferred to road, and what mail was carried was in the care of the DMU guards. In the 1950s the Butlin's trains were provided with stock from various sources, frequently vintage pieces that were in store for the winter months. It was not uncommon to see complete trains of Eastern Region 'Gresley' stock working from Huddersfield, and for two successive seasons in 1950 and 1951, on the peak summer Saturday covering the August Bank Holiday week-end, two Bullied coaches resplendent in malachite green were attached to a regular morning working at Chester, the circuit stock to Bangor being extended to Penychain and returning the same afternoon. It is believed that the vehicles were strengthening coaches on the Margate to Birkenhead working and detached at Chester, and which were worked back to the Southern Region the following Monday. Western Region coaches appeared over the line as a matter of course, and for a couple of seasons LNER corridor stock was to be seen in train make up.

In post war years, only two non-corridor three coach sets were regularly used. Set 1207 working the 5/45am to Pwllheli on Monday, Wednesday and Friday and the 2/52pm also to Pwllheli on Tuesdays, Thursdays and Saturdays, whilst Set 1232 worked the 2/52pm on Mondays Wednesdays and Fridays, and the 5.45am on Tuesdays, Thursdays and Saturdays. The pattern varied little until the workings were taken over by DMU's.

Caernarvon, Waterloo Port. June 1952. Fairburn 2-6-4T No.**42259** at the head of a six coach set, coasts the remaining mile into Caernarvon station with the 5/39pm Bangor to Afonwen. This train was always well patronised and the regular formation usually comprised six coaches. Waterloo Port Crossing was worked by a family who resided in the adjoining cottage and who were required to open the gates for road traffic whatever the time of day. The gates were normally set for the railway, protected by signals in each direction, the Down distant for the crossing giving indication to the traincrew. The combination of signals, straight road and clear sighting of the crossing coupled with the slight down grade enabled a minute to be picked up by keeping steam on up to this point. Drivers were required to whistle up at Pandy Lane Crossing to warn the Waterloo Port crossing keeper but normally steam was shut off at the crossing distant for the run in to the station. An unofficial warning of the imminence of Caernarvon station was the 'roaring rails' at this point. As the loco had been in traffic for some time, fireman usually pulled the coal in the bunker forward at this point.
W.G. Rear.

Griffiths Crossing. Wednesday, 13th April 1966. Fourteen years on, and slightly closer to Bangor than the previous picture, a Met.Cam. 2-car DMU working the 1920 Bangor to Caernarvon passes the site of the former Griffiths Crossing station. The signals protected the level crossing and the gates were normally set for the railway and against road traffic. The former Station Master's house is visible on the Up side. Today, the building remains, but the trackbed has been partly swept away by road improvements. The line between Menai Bridge and Caernarvon was singled shortly after this date with the lifting of the Down line.
A.Wyn Hobson

Special Workings.

Inevitably there were extra-special workings over the line from time to time, beyond the excursion and private charter trains, of which visits by Royalty to the area were the most noteworthy. The Special Arrangements for the Investiture of the Princes of Wales in 1911 and 1969 were probably the most complex, and although the latter is outside the strict sphere of this work, is nevertheless worthy of mention. In both events, Royalty detrained at Griffiths Crossing and travelled by road into Caernarvon so that the public would get the opportunity of seeing the participants at close quarters along the route to the castle where the ceremony was to take place. Since Griffith Crossing is two miles from Caernarvon the route to the outskirts of the town could have been somewhat lonely, although it is likely that the route was thronged with the populace for most of its route. In the case of the 1969 Investiture, the original Griffiths Crossing station had long closed and the platforms removed, so a temporary platform was erected adjacent to the Ferodo Works, slightly closer to town. Also, the Military were prominent, lining either side of the road into town, and because of the upsurge in patriotism, coupled with some resentment by the more extreme elements, security was much tighter.

The LNWR produced a special leaflet for the public wishing to travel to Caernarvon on Thursday July 13th 1911. An example of this document, designated C.& H. No.389, is owned by Tom Sherratt, who kindly made a copy available to the author. This states that the ordinary service of trains between Chester and Holyhead and Carnarvon was considerably altered on the day.

Twenty six trains arrived at Caernarvon from Menai Bridge from Bangor and stations east and from Anglesey. After the celebrations, six local of semi local trains arrived, interspersed with the exodus of returning specials

L. & N. W. R.

INVESTITURE
OF H.R.H.

The Prince of Wales
AT

CARNARVON,
ON

THURSDAY, JULY 13, 1911.

The ordinary service of Main Line Trains between Chester and Holyhead and Carnarvon will be considerably altered, and the revised service will be as shewn herein.

For alterations on Branch Lines see separate announcements.

Euston Station, London.   FRANK REE, General Manager.

Public traffic between Bangor and Caernarvon ceased about 10.00am and it is probable that the special trains carrying dignitaries, overseas special guests, and Royalty then occupied the Down line. Sadly no details of these workings have emerged. Doubtless the train carrying the British Royal family would have been the last to arrive, although it would have worked from Griffiths Crossing to Caernarvon as Empty Stock. Empty Stock workings to clear the station, with its three through and two bay platforms available would have ensured almost total line occupancy between Caernarvon and Menai Bridge. Probably main line stock was worked as far afield as Llandudno Junction and Holyhead for servicing, with corresponding empty workings back to Caernarvon in time to take up their return paths. There would have been a high degree of local

CAERNARVON
1911 Investiture Traffic

Arrivals at Caernarvon	From	dep arr	Bangor dep	dep	M.Bridge dep	Notes
4.05	Chester	2.10	3.40	3.45	-	
4.38	Chester	2.35	4.15	4.20	-	
5.40	Chester	3.50	5.18	5.23	-	
6.00	Llandudno Junction	5.10	5.40	5.43	-	Calls Llanfairfechan only
6.10	Llandudno Junction	5.20	5.50	5.53	-	Calls Bangor only
6.20	Llandudno Junction	5.33	-	-	-	Calls Penmaenmawr only
6.30	Llandudno Junction	5.45	-	-	-	Calls Conway only
6.40	Rhyl	5.33	6.18	6.23	-	Calls Bangor only
6.50	Rhyl	5.43	6.28	6.33	-	Calls Bangor only
7.00	Sandicroft	4.54	-	-	-	Calls all stations to Rhyl, then Colwyn Bay only
7.10	Gaerwen	6.38	-	-	6.50	possibly from Red Wharf Bay
7.25	Valley	6.10	-	-	7.00	
7.43	Gaerwen	7.10	-	-	7.22	possibly from Amlwch
7.52	Holyhead	6.45	-	-	-	possibly reverse at Bangor
8.00	Chester	6.00	7.38	7.45	-	Calls Rhyl and Bangor only
8.10	Chester	6.08	7.48	7.53	-	Calls Llandudno Junction and Bangor only
8.15	Llandudno Junction	7.28	-	-	-	Calls Conway, Penmaenmawr, Llanfairfechan only
8.25	Colwyn Bay	7.20	8.04	8.07	-	Calls Llandudno Junction, Conway and Bangor only
8.33	Rhyl	6.55	8.10	8.13	-	Calls most station to Llan. Jn. then Bangor only
8.48	Llandudno Junction	7.50	-	-	-	Calls Conway, Penmaenmawr Llanfairfechan and Aber only
9.02	Chester	5.50	8.41	8.50	8.56	Calls all stations
9.08	Chester	7.00	-	-	-	Calls Rhyl, Llandudno Junction only
9.24	Colwyn Bay	8.05	8.58	-	-	Calls all stations except Aber and Menai Bridge
9.37	Chester	7.35	-	-	-	Calls Llandudno Junction only
9.45	Rhyl	9.07	-	-	-	Calls all stations except Foryd, Llysfaen, Aber & M. Bridge
9.55	Chester	7.50	-	-	-	Calls Rhyl and Llandudno Junction only
5/42	Bangor	5/15	-	5/15	5/19	
6/28	Bangor	6/10	-	6/10	-	
7/49	Bangor	7/25	-	7/25	-	
8/21	Chester	6/10	7/55	8/05	8/10	
9/46	Bangor	9/25	-	9/25	-	
11/35	Bangor	11/15	-	11/15	-	

non-corridor stock sets working from Mold, Corwen and Denbigh, Blaenau Festiniog and Anglesey some of which would have been parked in the coal yard until required.

In the opposite direction, three trains departed Caernarvon for Bangor and beyond prior to the line closing to public traffic. After the ceremony and presumably after the Specials had departed, the service in the Up direction became intensive as the following table shows.

It is understood that the upper and lower goods yards were cleared of stock by the previous evening and freight traffic on the day was suspended. Temporary passenger platforms were erected in the goods yard. A second footbridge was built at the Bangor end, which connected North Road with the main platforms. This was removed

after only a few years.

According to the late J.M. Dunn, traffic between Afonwen and Caernarvon was worked on the day by Cambrian engines and men, who had learnt the road especially for the occasion although the Cambrian Railways had held reciprocal running powers over the line almost from the outset. The number of trains involved has not been discovered. It is possible that these trains worked into the temporary platforms in the goods yard, although another suggestion was that trains from Afonwen terminated short of Caernarvon Tunnel at the foot of the castle. Trains from Llanberis were worked by engine and men from the small shed there, worked into the Llanberis bay in the main station, which would not affect station working.

Dep C/von	To	due	M.Br arr	Bangor arr	dep	Notes
7.25	Chester	9.55	7.44	7.48	7.50	Calls principal stations
8.13	Chester	10.16	8.35	8.40	8.45	Calls Llandudno Junction only
9.25	Chester	11.40	9.48	9.52	10.00	Calls all stations to Llan. Jn, then Colwyn Bay only
5/15	Llandudno Jn	6/05	5/30	5/33	5/35	Calls all stations except Aber
5/35	Llandudno Jn	6/20	5/51	5/54	5/57	Calls Menai Bridge, Bangor, Penmaenmawr only
5/45	Chester	7/37	-	-	-	Calls Llandudno Junction, Colwyn Bay, Rhyl only
5/50	Euston	-	-	-	-	No stops shown but probably Crewe for loco purposes
5/55	Chester	8/40	6/16	6/19	6/25	Calls most stations except Mochdre, Llysfaen, Foryd, Talacre, Mostyn,
6/00	Llandudno Jn	7/10	6/26	6/30	6/33	Calls all stations
6/10	Rhyl	7/55	6/36	6/40	6/43	Calls most stations to Llan.Jn. except Conway, then C/Bay and Abergele only
6/40	Llandudno Jn	7/40	7/01	7/04	7/08	Calls all stations except Aber
6/50	Liverpool	-	-	-	-	Calls Llandudno Junction,Colwyn Bay, Rhyl and Chester (9/00pm) only
6/58	Birmingham	-	-	7/20	7/22	Calls Bangor, Llandudno Junction, Colwyn Bay, Rhyl and Chester (9/45pm) only
7/05	Llandudno Jn	8/08	7/23	7/26	7/29	Calls all stations
7/20	Llandudno Jn	8/15	7/37	7/40	7/43	Calls all stations except Aber
7/30	Manchester.	-	-	-	-	Calls Llandudno Junction, Colwyn Bay, Rhyl and Chester (9/35pm) only
7/38	Llandudno Jn	8/31	7/54	7/57	8/00	Calls all stations except Aber
7/45	Chester	9/55	-	8/04	8/06	Calls Bangor, Llandudno Junction, Colwyn Bay and Rhyl only
7/50	Llandudno Jn	8/50	8/07	8/10	8/13	Calls all stations except Aber
8/05	Llandudno Jn	9/00	8/22	8/25	8/28	Calls all stations except Aber
8/15	Chester	10/25	8/33	8/37	8/40	Calls Bangor, Llanfairfechan, Penmaenmawr, Llan.Jn., C/Bay and Rhyl only
8/25	Crewe	-	8/42	8/45	9/10	Calls Bangor, Llandudno Junction, Colwyn Bay, Rhyl, Flint & Chester (11/05pm)
8/45	Llandudno Jn	9/50	9/11	9/14	9/20	Calls all stations except Aber
9/08	Chester &GW	11/15	-	9/33	9/36	Calls Bangor, Rhyl and Chester (11/15pm) only
9/15	Llandudno	10/35	9/37	9/40	9/43	Calls all stations
9/40	Llandudno Jn	10/43	10/01	10/04	10/09	Calls all stations
9/55	Birkenhead	-	-	10/18	10/21	Calls Bangor, Llandudno Junction, Colwyn Bay, Rhyl and Chester (12.05am) only
10/00	Rhyl	11/45	-	10/25	10/28	Calls all stations except Aber, Llysfaen and Foryd
10/20	Sandicroft	12.32	-	10/37	10/40	Calls Bangor, Rhyl only, then all stations.
10/35	Llandudno Jn	11/29	-	10/54	10/58	Calls all stations except Menai Bridge and Aber
10/50	Denbigh & Mold	-	-	11/10	11/13	Calls Bangor, Llandudno Junction, Colwyn Bay and Rhyl (12.13am) only
10/55	Chester	1.20	11/17	11/20	11/24	Calls all stations except Conway,Llandulas & Foryd to Rhyl (12.42) then Chester
11/05	Rhyl	12/45	11/25	11/29	11/32	Calls all stations to Llandudno Junction then Colwyn Bay and Abergele only
11/30	Denbigh & Corwen	-	-	11/48	11/52	Calls Bangor, Llandudno Junction, Colwyn Bay and Rhyl (12.45am) only

Caernarvon Shed

A set of Engine and Men's Workings commencing 8th July 1929 survives. By this time most prestige work had been lost to Bangor. Locomotives nominally based at Caernarvon shed were included with the Bangor allocation, and most maintenance was done there. Only those minor repairs necessary to keep engines on the road were effected at the shed.

In common with all LMS sheds, the diagrammed work at this time was designed Passenger (or Freight) Engine Workings. Despite the fact that the work was specified for passenger work, Freight engines were rostered in many cases.

PASSENGER ENGINE WORKINGS

Turn 1 — ONE CLASS 2 FREIGHT TANK ENGINE (COAL)

Days	Class	Dep	From	To	Arr
S	Pass	6.45am	Caernarvon	Bangor	7.07am
S	Pass	7.45am	Bangor	Llandudno Junction	8.22am
S	Pass	10.24am	Llandudno Junction	Llanberis	11.25am
S	Frt	1/00pm	Llanberis	Caernarvon	2/15pm
S	Pass	4/25pm	Caernarvon	Bangor	4/49pm
S	Pass	6/55pm	Bangor	Afonwen	8/20pm
ThPass		9/00pm	Afonwen	Caernarvon	10/20pm
ThO	Pass	8/40pm	Afonwen	Caernarvon	9/34pm
		SHUNT		"	11/00pm
SO	Pass	7.05am	Caernarvon	Bangor	7.27am
SO	Pass	7.45am	Bangor	Llandudno Junction	8.22am
SO	Pass	10.00am	Llandudno Junction	Llandudno	10.10am
SO	LE		Llandudno	Llandudno Junction	
SO	Pass	11.17am	Llandudno Junction	Bangor	11.37am
SO		SHUNT		"	
SO	Pass	2/00pm	Bangor	Caernarvon	2/22pm
		RELIEF 2/25PM			
SO	Pass	2/35pm	Caernarvon	Bangor	2/57pm
SO		SHUNT		"	
SO	Pass	5/45pm	Bangor	Caernarvon	6/07pm
SO		SHUNT		"	9/00pm
SO	Frt	9/10pm	Caernarvon	Menai Bridge	9/30pm
SO	LE		Menai Bridge	Caernarvon	

Turn 2 — ONE CLASS 2 FREIGHT TANK ENGINE (COAL) (off Turn 1F)

Days	Class	Dep	From	To	Arr
D	Pass	3/35pm	Caernarvon	Bangor	3/57pm
D		SHUNT		"	
D	Pass	5/08pm	Bangor	Llandudno Junction	5/41pm
D	Pass	6/17pm	Llandudno Junction	Llandudno	6/26pm
D	LE		Llandudno	Llandudno Junction	
D	Pass	7/20pm	Llandudno Junction	Bangor	7/50pm
D		SHUNT		"	8/45pm
S	Pass	9/00		Caernarvon	9/23pm
ThO	Pass	10/00pm	Caernarvon	Bangor	10/22pm
ThO	Pass	10/40pm	Bangor	Caernarvon	11/01pm
SO	Pass	9/20pm	Caernarvon	Bangor	9/44pm
SO	Pass	9/55pm	Caernarvon	Nantlle	10/27pm
SO	ECS	10/35pm	Nantlle	Caernarvon	10/58pm

Turn 3 — ONE CLASS 2 FREIGHT TANK ENGINE (COAL)

Days	Class	Dep	From	To	Arr
D	Pass	11.15am	Caernarvon	Bangor	11.37am
S	Pass	1/18pm	Bangor	Caernarvon	1/40pm
SO	Pass	1/23pm	Bangor	Caernarvon	1/45pm
D	Cpld	3/30pm	Caernarvon	Llanberis	3/57pm
D	Pass	5/10pm	Llanberis	Caernarvon	5/28pm
D		SHUNT		"	6/00pm

Turn 4 — ONE CLASS 2 FREIGHT TANK ENGINE (COAL)

Days	Class	Dep	From	To	Arr
S	Frt	3/50pm	Caernarvon	Menai Bridge	4/10pm
S	LE		Menai Bridge	Bangor	
S	Pass	5/45pm	Bangor	Caernarvon	6/07pm
S	LE	6/40pm	Caernarvon	Llanberis	7/20pm
S	Pass	7/30pm	Llanberis	Caernarvon	7/51pm
S	LE		Caernarvon	Penygroes	
S	Frt	8/50pm	Penygroes	Caernarvon	9/20pm
S		SHUNT		"	10/20pm

Turn 5 — ONE CLASS 2 FREIGHT TANK ENGINE (COAL)

Days	Class	Dep	From	To	Arr
S	Pass	10.00am	Caernarvon	Bangor	10.22am
S	LE		Bangor	Menai Bridge	
S.	Frt	12/15pm	Menai Bridge	Caernarvon	12/35pm
S		SHUNT		"	4/35pm
SO	Pass	10.00am	Caernarvon	Bangor	10.22am
SO	Frt	11.38am	Bangor	Menai Bridge	11.48am
SO		SHUNT		" "	
SO	Frt	2/55pm	Menai Bridge	Caernarvon	3/15pm
SO		SHUNT		"	4/30pm
SO	Pass	8/30pm	Caernarvon	Nantlle	9/03pm
SO	Pass	9/13pm	Nantlle	Caernarvon	9/45pm
SO	Pass	10/00pm	Caernarvon	Bangor	10/22pm
SO	Pass	10/40pm	Bangor	Caernarvon	11/01pm

Turn 6 — ONE CLASS 2 FREIGHT TANK ENGINE

Days	Class	Dep	From	To	Arr
D	Frt	5.40am	Caernarvon	Llanberis	6/45am
D	Pass	7.20am	Llanberis	Caernarvon	7.41am
D	Pass	7.45am	Caernarvon	Llanberis	8.10am
D	Pass	8.18am	Llanberis	Caernarvon	8.39am
D	Pass	9.25am	Caernarvon	Llanberis	9.52am
D	Pass	9.55am	Llanberis	Caernarvon	10.17am

Turn 6 (continued)

Days	Class	Dep	From	To	Arr
D	Pass	12/15pm	Caernarvon	Llanberis	12/42pm
D	Pass	12/50pm	Llanberis	Caernarvon	1/11pm
SO	Pass	1/25pm	Caernarvon	Llanberis	1/52pm
SO	Pass	2/00pm	Llanberis	Caernarvon	2/21pm
D	Pass	2/35pm	Caernarvon	Llanberis	3/02pm
D	Pass	3/05pm	Llanberis	Caernarvon	3/26pm
D	Pass	3/30pm	Caernarvon	Llanberis	3/57pm
D	Pass	4/00pm	Llanberis	Caernarvon	4/21pm
SO	Pass	4/35pm	Caernarvon	Llanberis	5/02pm
SO	Pass	5/25pm	Llanberis	Caernarvon	5/46pm
D	Pass	6/10pm	Caernarvon	Llanberis	6/37pm
D	Pass	6/55pm	Llanberis	Bangor	7/41pm
D	Pass	8/00pm	Bangor	Llanberis	8/57pm
S	LE	9/05pm	Llanberis	Caernarvon	9/26pm
SO	Pass	9/05pm	Llanberis	Caernarvon	9/26pm
SO	Pass	10/00pm	Caernarvon	Llanberis	10/27pm
SO	LE	10/35pm	Llanberis	Caernarvon	10/56pm

Turn 8 — ONE CLASS 2 FREIGHT TANK ENGINE (COAL)

Days	Class	Dep	From	To	Arr
D	Frt	6.10am	Caernarvon	Nantlle	7.10am
D	Pass	7.25am	Nantlle	Penygroes	7.30am
D	Pass	7.40am	Penygroes	Nantlle	7.45am
D	Pass	8.10am	Nantlle	Penygroes	8.15am
D	Pass	8.25am	Penygroes	Nantlle	8.30am
D	Pass	9.40am	Nantlle	Penygroes	9.45am
D	Pass	10.00am	Penygroes	Nantlle	10.05am
D	Pass	11.25am	Nantlle	Penygroes	11.30am
D	Pass	11.45am	Penygroes	Nantlle	11.50am
D	Pass	12.20pm	Nantlle	Penygroes	12/25pm
		RELIEF 12/32pm (S)			
		1st set home passenger per 12/58pm ex Penygroes			
		2nd set as passenger per 12/07pm ex Caernarvon			
D	Pass	12/35pm	Penygroes	Nantlle	12/40pm
SO	Pass	1/05pm	Nantlle	Caernarvon	1/34pm
		RELIEF 1/34pm (SO)			
SO	Pass	1/40pm	Caernarvon	Nantlle	2/08pm
D	Pass	2/15pm	Nantlle	Penygroes	2/20pm
D	Pass	2/35pm	Penygroes	Nantlle	2/40pm
D	Pass	2/45pm	Nantlle	Penygroes	2/50pm
D	Pass	3/00pm	Penygroes	Nantlle	3/05pm
D	Frt	3/40pm	Nantlle	Penygroes	3/45pm
D	LE	4/10pm	Penygroes	Nantlle	4/15pm
D	Pass	4/25pm	Nantlle	Penygroes	4/30pm
D	Pass	4/50pm	Penygroes	Nantlle	4/55pm
D	Pass	5/35pm	Nantlle	Penygroes	5/40pm
D	Pass	5/50pm	Penygroes	Nantlle	5/55pm
D	Pass	6/05pm	Nantlle	Penygroes	6/10pm
D	Pass	6/20pm	Penygroes	Nantlle	6/25pm
D	Pass	6/30pm	Nantlle	Penygroes	6/35pm
D	Pass	6/45pm	Penygroes	Nantlle	6/50pm
D	Pass	7/25pm	Nantlle	Penygroes	7/30pm
D	Pass	8/00pm	Penygroes	Nantlle	8/05pm
D	Pass	8/20pm	Nantlle	Penygroes	8/25pm
D	LE	8/27pm	Penygroes	Caernarvon	8/47pm

Turn 9 — ONE CLASS 2 FREIGHT TANK ENGINE (COAL)

Days	Class	Dep	From	To	Arr
S	Pass	11.35am	Caernarvon	Llanberis	11.55am
S	Frt	1/00pm	Llanberis	Caernarvon	2/15pm
S	Frt	3/50pm	Caernarvon	Menai Bridge	4/10pm
S		SHUNT 5/25pm		"	
S	LE		Menai Bridge	Caernarvon	

FREIGHT ENGINE WORKINGS

Turn 1F — TWO CLASS 4 FREIGHT ENGINES (STANDARD)

Days	Class	Dep	From	To	Arr
MO	Frt	3.50am	Caernarvon	Mold Junction	8.16am
S	Frt	10/40pm	Caernarvon	Mold Junction	3.45am
		Engine also works Mold Junction Turn 23.F			
		BOOK OFF			
FS	Frt	11/50pm	Mold Junction	Caernarvon	4.10am
FO	Frt	11/50pm	Mold Junction	Caernarvon	5.25am
SO	Frt	5/50pm	Mold Junction	Caernarvon	10/05pm

Turn 3F — ONE CLASS 2 FREIGHT TANK ENGINE (COAL)

Days	Class	Dep	From	To	Arr
D	Sht	4.30am	Caernarvon		11.20am
S		RELIEF 11.20am			
S	Frt	12/20pm	Caernarvon	Dinas Junction	12/45pm
S	Frt	1/40pm	Dinas Junction	Caernarvon	1/55pm
S		2/00pm SHUNT		"	6/30pm

Afonwen. 25th July 1949. This view shows how close the sea came up to Afonwen station, and whilst passengers saw it as an idyllic spot in the warm summer months, the miles of empty sands tempting the weary traveller, few saw it with a winter gale blowing the spray off the Cardigan Bay and drenching passengers and railway workers alike. At least the passengers could seek shelter, but the shunters and platform staff had to endure the elements. Machynlleth's 2-6-2 No.4560 drifts into the station with the 1/35pm from Dovey Junction to Pwllheli. The valves are lifting as the brakes are applied. The Up platform was extended in the late 1930's to accommodate longer trains and this view shows where the extension commenced, with the paving slabs giving way to a plain tarmac surface. At one time a short siding butted up to the platform ramp, but this was removed about this time. The sidings on the Down side, with a few mineral wagons resident, look slightly overgrown, but in all probability this was due to the late arrival of the weed-killer train which toured the line annually. Note the young man in the once traditional striped school cap and short trousers sitting on the seat, which date this photograph.   *H.B. Priestley.*

Afonwen. 5th August 1948. A sea mist hangs over the water as 4-4-0 No.9012 trundles through Afonwen on the Down line but in the Up direction with a Class K freight from Pwllheli to Portmadoc! Stock for a Caernarvon-bound train stands in the Up platform, and more stock stands on the Up Goods line to the right of the picture. In all probability the Up passenger loop platform will shortly be occupied by a passenger working to Barmouth. Notice the barrow full of parcels awaiting loading into the guards van when the train arrives, lurking outside the licenced Restaurant Room can be seen a bowler hatted official keeping a watchful eye on the proceedings. Just visible between the footbridge ramp and the carriage sides can be seen the two two-arm bracket signals protecting the Down Caernarvon line and the Up line from Pwllheli.
H.B. Priestley.

Afonwen. 19th August 1954. The 4-4-0 'Dukedog' class locomotives were the mainstay of the Cambrian Coast line for many years, having been introduced to the line in the late 1930's. Several examples of the class spent their entire lives on the line, and were held with great affection by traincrews, apart from when it was necessary to work tender-first in inclement weather. Here **9016** from Portmadoc shed stands in the Up passenger loop platform with LMS stock. Possibly this was the 3/35pm from Pwllheli to Bangor, which would be worked forward by a Bangor engine and crew, whilst the Portmadoc men would hook off and draw clear, to await their next working. The stationmaster lived on the site, not in the station building, but occupied the bungalow alongside the Up Goods loop. His hedge and front gate can just be seen in the photograph and, apart from the single line of track, this property is the only surviving relic of the once extensive complex of Afonwen.   *H.B.Priestley.*

Afonwen. 19th August 1954. The Cambrian Coast line was restricted to locomotives of Blue, Yellow or uncoloured classification, which limited motive power to the smaller types, although the 'Manor' class were on the approved list. Between Afonwen and Pwllheli, LMS Class 5 4-6-0 were authorised and were to be seen on summer Saturdays until the Caernarvon line closed. The Western Region were restricted to a few classes, including the 'Dukedogs' including C.B. Collett's taper boiler Class 2201 0-6-0, the 43xx Class 2-6-0 and the 45XX 2-6-2 tank engines which gradually replaced the pre-group designs. Here No.**3207** stands at the Up passenger loop platform with the 9.35am a class 'A' working to Machynlleth, which included through coaches for Paddington, hence the two lamp headcode on the bufferbeam. Midweek there were only a couple of Class 'A' workings along part or all of the Cambrian Coast line.

H.B. Priestley.

Afonwen. 20th August 1954. Former Cambrian Railways 0-6-0, No.849 in the GWR stock list, was one of three remaining pre-group standard gauge design to survive, although by this time its days were numbered. It s seen here drawing into Afonwen Up platform with a Pwllheli to Barmouth Class 'B' working. The station building was narrow, and this was emphasised by the pitch of the roof and four tall chimneys. The canopy, which extended to the platform edge gave some shelter, but only when carriages were standing at the platform which intercepted the wind and rain that blew in off the sea. A few passengers wait expectantly, and a barrow load of parcels are ready for loading into the leading guards van. On the extreme right of the picture can be seen the licenced Refreshment Room, managed for many years by an elderly lady who depended on the traincrew and platform staff for trade for most of the year. Coaching stock can be seen through the smoke and steam in the ashpit siding by the water tanks on the Down side. These would not stand there for long, probably only until the evening when they would be worked forward to Pwllheli and the exodus from Butlin's Camp the following day. *H.B. Priestley.*

Afonwen. 20th August 1954. Cambrian 0-6-0 No.849 towards the end of its working life and 'Swindonised' stands in the Up platform with the 1/35pm Pwllheli to Portmadoc working. These engines were rough riding, and it was believed by the powers-that-be that the balancing of the driving wheels was at fault. To remedy this, holes were drilled in the balance weights, but didn't improve things very much. Despite this weakness, most enginemen preferred them to some of the more modern replacements and they ended their days working passenger or freight duties at random. Behind the front bufferbeam can be seen the chimney of the station master's house, screened from view by a thick hedge although passengers (and staff) on the footbridge could look over, and rarely were staff caught relaxing and off guard. *H.B. Priestley.*

Afonwen. 1954. Afonwen station was one of those rarities - a junction station built solely to effect changes of route. Like Bala Junction there was no public road access to the station although, unlike Bala Junction, Afonwen was advertised in public and working time tables. The LNWR, LMS and London Midland Region had running powers over the GWR tracks from the junction, through the platform roads and goods lines. The Up passenger loop seen here was nominally regarded as the 'foreigner's' platform, although LM trains worked to and from all platforms according to traffic requirements. The Up passenger loop and Up goods line were rarely photographed, possibly due to the angle of sunlight, which cast the buildings in shadow for most days and most of the day. Public access was along an unmade road from the cluster of buildings half a mile away on the Pwllheli to Portmadoc road, and few people ever had cause to use the footbridge at the western end of the station, which provided this view. The station master's house juts out into a field, and is partially hidden behind a hedge, which also screened the building from the rough weather in winter which blew in off the sea. The main station building with its four stacks looks in need of attention, as slate cladding on the gable end has become dislodged in places. The manhole in the foreground was also a convenient marker for train crews to deposit the ash and clinker from the firebox when cleaning out the fire. The deposits were scattered over the footpath over the years although from time to time the permanent way gangs lifted the material for use elsewhere around the station.   *J.H. Moss.*

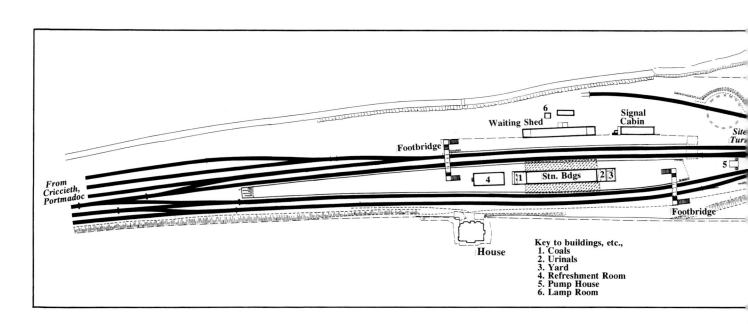

Key to buildings, etc.,
1. Coals
2. Urinals
3. Yard
4. Refreshment Room
5. Pump House
6. Lamp Room

AFONWEN

Afonwen. c.1954. Probably the most informative view taken of the west end of Afonwen station, from the footbridge mentioned in the previous caption. In the foreground stand two cars which would today be worth a small fortune as vintage machines. The private road to the station extends into the distance, following the course of the track over the Afon Wen from which the station gets its name. The three platform roads were signalled for bi-directional working and the Up passenger loop Down direction starter arm is just visible on the extreme left hand edge of the picture. At the foot of the platform ramp in front of the small hut which housed the water pumping equipment for filling the water tanks, is the Up platform Down direction starter, with route indicator below the lower quadrant arm. The furthest line is the former turntable road, that passed under the twin water tanks. After removal of the turntable in the 1930's, the line was used as a suitable point where engines on layover time could clean the fire. The siding was also used as a short term refuge for parking coaching stock, although this was kept clear throughout Saturdays during the summer months. Access to the turntable road, (also called the ashpit road) was off the Down main line, which extended as far as the river bank, providing additional storage space. Adjacent to this line were the employees cottages. In the distance can be seen the extensive development of Butlin's Camp. In front of the cottages can be seen a facing crossover, which replaced a scissors crossover in the late 1930's, beyond that another trailing crossover. Two tracks cross the bridge over the river before the routes diverge, the line to Pwllheli falling away to the left whilst the Caernarvon line bears right and commences the climb towards Chwilog. Two two-arm bracket signals protect the approaches to the station.
J.H. Moss.

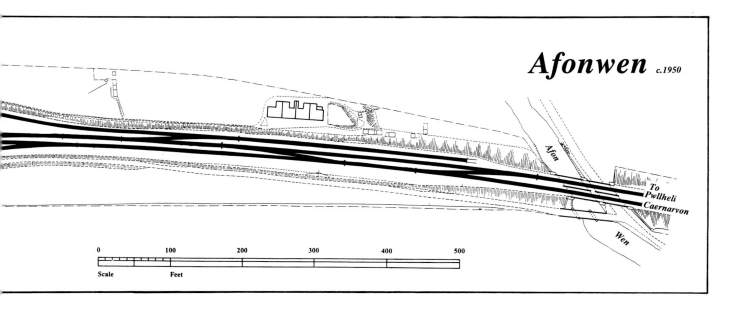

Afonwen c.1950

Afonwen. n.d. Views of the turntable at Afonwen are exceedingly rare and this is the only one to have surfaced over many years. The quality of the print is indifferent but is included for its unique value. Here Cambrian Railways 2-4-0 No.**10** is being turned in readiness for its next turn of duty. The turntable was not an easy one to use, and it was frequently necessary to summon assistance from platform staff with the push, as seen here. The pit was at the water's edge, and frequently it was necessary to dig out the shingle and sand prior to turning. The LNWR and later the LMS used the turntable, for which the latter paid a charge, and when the GWR decided to remove it and withdraw the facility, it was offered to the LMS who declined to take up the offer. This had consequences for the LMS who used tender engines on their workings from Bangor, and even the directorate softened their hearts at the thought of twenty seven miles of tender first running in bad weather. The locomotive was built by Beyer, Peacock in 1864, works number 422, for the West Midland Railway, and which passed into GWR ownership, who numbered it 213, and it was sold it out of service in 1911 to A.R. Angus, for signalling experiments on the West Somerset Mineral Railway. It was acquired from the Bute Docks Supply Company in 1921 and given diagram number 18. On resuming GWR ownership it was allocated the new number 1328. Note the position of the ownership high on the tender sides. *Collection W.G. Rear.*

Afonwen. 11th September 1894. Cambrian Railways 2-4-0 No.**55** stands at the eastern end of Afonwen station with a passenger working to Portmadoc standing at the Up platform. Passengers for Down trains to Pwllheli were obliged to cross the tracks by the barrow crossing. There was only a rudimentary shelter on the platform, with no provision for heating. In winter, the practice was to stay in the waiting room on the Up side until the train was approaching and make a dash across the tracks at the last minute. Whilst there is no record of any accident, there must have been a few 'near misses' and subsequently a footbridge was provided, which placed the barrow crossing out of bounds to the public. This locomotive and others in its class were the mainstay of passenger services along the coast for many years, and No.55 passed into Great Western ownership to become No.1333. A note on the photograph gives the fireman as Morris Evans. *courtesy E.M. Johnson.*

Afonwen. 1960. In 1954 the Cambrian Coast line motive power was modernised by the introduction of British Railways Standard Class 2MT 2-6-0 locomotives, replacing the older Cambrian Railways 0-6-0's, and some GWR 2-6-2T and 0-6-0 locomotives. This modernisation was a mixed blessing to the traincrews. For the first time they had enclosed cabs which gave adequate protection against the vagaries of the weather. Conversely the locomotives were regarded as less powerful than some of the designs they replaced and in turn some of these newcomers were themselves replaced by Class 3MT 2-6-2T of the class 82xxx series, these in turn by the 80xxx Class 4 2-6-4T which proved ideal for the length of line run. However not all the 78xxx disappeared, and a couple survived and performed much useful work between Pwllheli and Machynlleth. Here No.**78003** attached to Portmadoc shed runs into the Up platform with the 5/30pm Pwllheli to Barmouth. The first vehicle is a mail van which will be transferred to a Chester working at Barmouth. Useful details for the modeller are shown of the footbridge which led to the unmade road providing access to and from the station. *G.H. Platt.*

Afonwen. c.1938. A 'vintage' photograph, judging by the fashions on display! One of the two water tanks on the turntable road dominates the skyline at the western end of the Down platform, enhanced by the extending shadows of the evening sun. A lamp post towers over the signal cabin, devoid of its lamp, but the windlass arrangement can be seen on the original photograph. An LMS suburban non corridor third coach stands in the Up platform road, no doubt waiting for the locomotive to run round the stock. In the far end of the turntable road stand two coaches parked for the following day's work. A double compound crossing from the Up to the Down line and turntable road can be made out beyond the platform ramp. In the distance stand the two two-arm bracket signals already mentioned. Beyond the furthest trailing crossover the two single lines run in parallel over the river bridge before diverging to Pwllheli and Caernarvon. *J.M. Dunn*

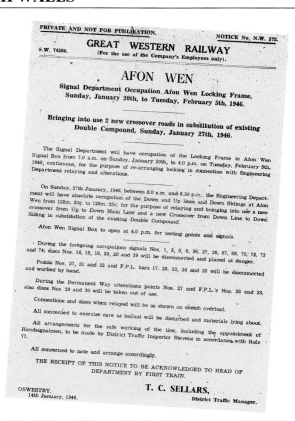

Afonwen. c.1938. This 4 arm lower quadrant bracket signal was installed at the eastern end of the Up platform at Afonwen after the platform was extended. LMS coaching stock occupies the Up side exchange sidings, parked for a few hours, but would have been cleared on two evening workings to Bangor. On the Down side, a sundry collection of freight wagons stand in the machine sidings awaiting uplifting by the next LMS freight trip to Menai Bridge.   *W.G. Rear collection.*

Afonwen. No date. With the closure of the line to Caernarvon in December 1964 Afonwen station lost its justification to remain open. It was no longer an interchange station, and the few houses (and laundry) that made up Afonwen village were some half a mile away on the main Crosville bus route between Portmadoc and Pwllheli did not provide sufficient revenue to warrant retention. The station continued to be listed in the working time tables for the line until 1970 but merely served as a block post for a couple of years. Ultimately the platforms and buildings were demolished and surplus track lifted This view was taken shortly after closure, and the only indication that trains no longer called at the station apart from the deserted appearance was the removal of the signal arms and the rails in the sidings and running lines no longer in use were starting to rust.

H. Townley, courtesy C. Bentley.

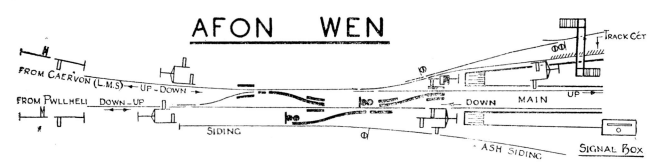

Afonwen. 1957. Diesel Multiple Units came to the North Wales coast lines in March 1956. After initial trials over the Afonwen and Amlwch lines, using Llandudno Junction men who needed piloting facilities, as they did not sign for the road, the units disappeared for a few months and were worked up the Conwy Valley line to Blaenau Ffestiniog. The brief incursion was, however, a warning and the following winter season saw four Bangor drivers train on the units and ultimately take over most services on the Amlwch line. The 12/20pm working from Bangor to Afonwen slotted into the DMU diagram, and became a new and popular feature. The most popular seat was behind the driver, who was scrutinised on his techniques by enthusiasts and the general public alike. The huge expanse of glass gave panoramic view of the country, hitherto unavailable, and boosted traffic accordingly. Here one of the early Derby 'Lightweight' Units stands in the Up platform with the 3/50pm to Bangor awaiting time. Driver V.N.B. Edwards was at the console and he was content, preferring the cleanliness of his new role, in isolation, to the dirty but accompanied life on a conventional steam footplate. On the Down line stands the stock of the 1/35pm from Dovey Junction to Pwllheli which connected with the Bangor working.   *J.H. Moss.*

Afonwen. n.d. Taken from the footbridge connecting the Island and Down platforms looking towards Pwllheli. The Down platform was a bleak cheerless affair, open to the elements, although mercifully with its back to the sea. The twin water tanks stand behind the platform on the former turntable road. On the Up platform, the original canopy was extended slightly, as can be seen here. Notice the arrangement for carrying away the rainwater from the roof, which led down to an open gully before disappearing down a grid by the gents urinals.

W.G. Rear collection.

Afonwen. 1957. This view shows some of the station furniture at the western end of the island platform, and apart from the pre-cast concrete bunker in the foreground, little changed over the years. although the water columns have been renewed with more modern swivel arms. Here No.**46430** of 6K (Rhyl) shed stands at the Up passenger loop platform topping up its tanks before continuing home through Caernarvon and Bangor with one of the two 'Land Cruise' workings that ran daily during the summer months. The Land Cruise workings started at Rhyl and Llandudno, the latter reversing at Rhyl. The two trains followed one another from Rhyl to Denbigh, Ruthin and Corwen, at about thirty minutes interval, where they gained Western Region tracks, and took the Ruabon to Barmouth Junction line through Bala Junction, and alongside Llyn Tegid, where drivers were required to keep speed to 25mph to exploit the scenery. The line then climbed to the summit at Garneddwen and descended down the Wnion valley to Dolgellau, thence along the estuary to Barmouth Junction, (latterly Morfa Mawddach) where they joined with the Cambrian Coast line. After crossing Barmouth viaduct the trains paused for ninety minutes to enable passengers to get off and briefly explore the town. Then it was back on board to continue at a leisurely pace

along Cardigan Bay through Harlech, Porthmadog and Criccieth to Afonwen where another brief halt was made to take on water. Then it was up the branch to Caernarvon, where yet another stop for water was made before continuing on the final leg of the journey through Menai Bridge, Bangor and Penmaenmawr. At Llandudno Junction the Llandudno train reversed direction for the short journey to its destination. The tour was extremely popular, and developed from modest beginnings in 1951, when it was titled 'The Festival Land Cruise Train'. The following year it was rechristened 'The Radio Land Cruise Train', complete with radio commentary given over loudspeakers throughout the journey. Originally only one train ran, but its popularity was such that a second train was introduced starting from Rhyl.   *J.H. Moss.*

Afonwen. 2nd August 1960. Collett 0-6-0 No.**2204** wearing an 89C (Machynlleth) shedplate pulls in to the Up platform at Afonwen with a train for Portmadoc. GWR design engines were still commonplace on the Cambrian Coast line, although many of the passenger workings were now in the hands of BR Standard Class 2 tender engines. On the Down side, the signal box dominates, and in winter provided limited shelter from the wind and spray that blew off the Cardigan Bay. It was one of the less attractive jobs that signalmen had to endure when delivering or receiving the single line token for trains off the Caernarvon line. Beyond the platform can be seen one of the two water tanks standing on the former turntable road.

D. Rutherford; N.E. Stead collection

Chwilog. n.d. Chwilog station buildings, looking towards Caernarvon. This view, taken before the Grouping, shows limited detail, but identifies standard LNWR practice. The station nameboard is made up to the basic 'Crewe' design. A small six lever frame stands at the head of the platform ramp, open to the elements. The frame only controlled signals and the level crossing locking mechanism. The station was a staff token point, although there was no provision for passenger trains to cross here. In the right foreground is the token dispenser with the receiving apparatus behind it. The equipment was rarely used, as all trains stopped here and tokens were exchanged in a civilised manner, by hand and on the platform. The token instruments were located in the station office.   *W.G. Rear collection.*

Chwilog. 1958. Looking along the platform towards Afonwen, this view shows the goods yard in some detail. Coal was the main inward freight traffic and one siding was devoted to this traffic, and used by local coal merchants, who weighed and bagged their product direct from the open wagons. Beyond the mineral wagon can be seen the small weighing machine office, found in almost every country goods yard on the system. The siding alongside the main line was used by the local agricultural co-operative society for loading and discharging their merchandise. They also had a shed alongside the coal siding. A pair of single gates straddle the line, normally held open for road traffic. These were hand operated, interlocked with the signals from the lever frame on the end of the platform. Immediately beyond the gates can be seen the turnout on the Down side to the milk traffic landing. From 1943 until 1949 five vans were loaded daily with milk churns for Hanson's Dairies, Broad Green, Liverpool, and traffic was worked throughout by Bangor men on one of their few surviving lodging turns. The siding could only accommodate five vans, and this inhibited development so much so that this business was diverted to road tankers, and ceased by the commencement of the winter season. Today the site has been cleared of all traces of the railway and a modern housing estate stands in its place.
J.H. Moss.

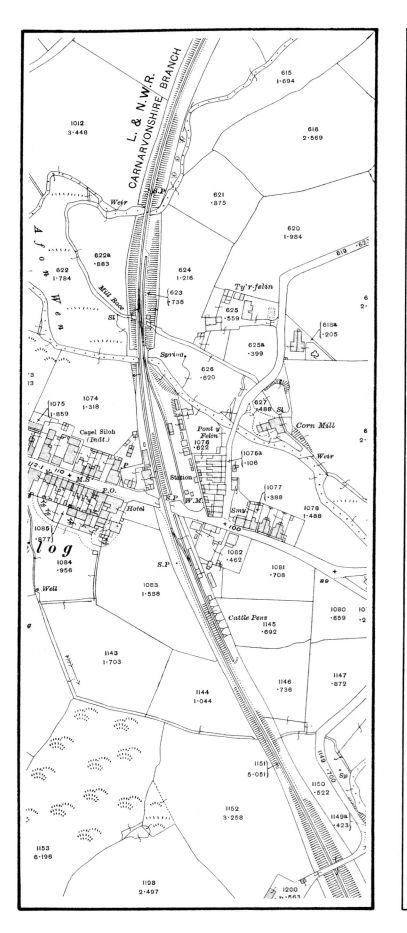

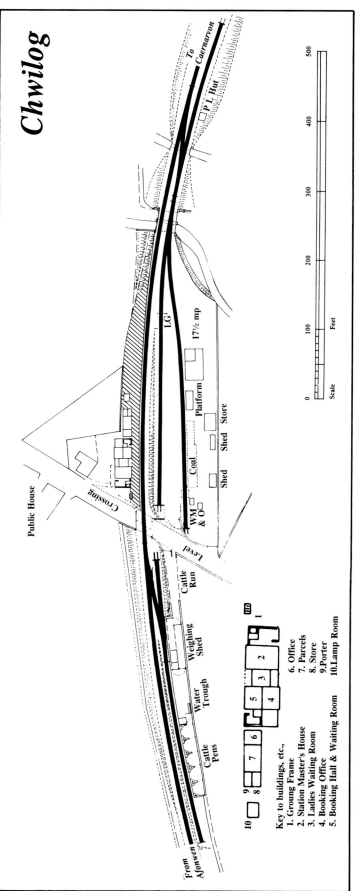

Chwilog

L. & N.W.R.
CARNARVONSHIRE BRANCH

To Caernarvon

P L Hut

17½ mp

Public House

Crossing

Level

From Afonwen

LG

Platform

WM & O

Coal Shed

Shed Store

Shed

Weighing Shed

Water Trough

Cattle Run

Cattle Pens

Key to buildings, etc.,
1. Groung Frame
2. Station Master's House
3. Ladies Waiting Room
4. Booking Office
5. Booking Hall & Waiting Room
6. Office
7. Parcels
8. Store
9. Porter
10. Lamp Room

Scale   Feet
0   100   200   300   400   500

Chwilog. May 1964. Another view of the impressive station building, taken from the goods yard. The buildings were out of proportion to the importance of the village, although the freight traffic generated here was considerably more than the passenger side of the business. At the time of the photograph, however, the line was under notice of closure, and the freight traffic had been killed off, hence the growth on the siding and stops. Beyond the main building were a collection of huts, used as goods store and private stores respectively. The gradient through the station was on a falling line towards Afonwen, although the goods siding was on the level. In the late 1950's the platform facing was decaying and in need of replacing, and this was completed in the winter of 1957, using pre cast concrete units. Notice the upper quadrant starter signal on a modern tubular post, with the distant for Afonwen mounted beneath the home arm. At the head of the platform ramp can be seen the LNWR six lever frame.

W.G. Rear.

Chwilog. July 1963. One of the last designs of locomotive to work over the branch were the British Railways Standard 3MT tank engines of 82xxx class, displaced from the Cambrian Coast line. One of the standard duties for Class 3 tank engines based at Bangor was the Up 'Welshman' working from Portmadoc, although by this time there was no valid reason for not using Class 4 2-6-4T engines, as the 80xxx series had been passed for working from Machynlleth to Pwllheli, and several were based at either shed as well as being the main source of motive power at Bangor. Here 82032 of 6H draws to a halt at the platform with the Saturday working of 'The Welshman' reporting number 1A42 and running under Class 'A' headlamps. The long staff has been exchanged for the token for the section of line to Brynkir, just visible in the door of the loco cab, whilst the porter signalman watches the train into the platform before returning the Up home signal to danger and opening the gates to road traffic. Passengers are sparse in number, an omen of the impending closure perhaps? The track in the goods yard is neglected and much overgrown. Notice the artistic work on the lineside, with the station name picked out in bricks, and whitewashed by the staff. *J.W.T. House.*

Chwilog. 1958. Four years earlier the scene was so different. The new platform facing gleams new for the photographer, the station furniture, though old is well maintained with not a weed in sight and in the distance, the fencing is freshly whitewashed, as is the brick built name on the embankment alongside the running line. The ballast is edged with clean stone and immaculately kept. Even the goods siding looks cared for, and there was still a lot of traffic to and from the yard at this time. The line climbs away towards Llangybi and keeps the fireman fully occupied for the next ten minutes. Under the arm of the loading gauge can be seen the Up Starter and the Down Home signal on the same post. The signal post was located beyond the goods yard point to enable shunting in the yard to come inside station limits. The points were controlled by Annett's key. *J.H. Moss.*

Llangybi. 1958. British Railways Standard Class 4MT 2-6-4 No.80094 of Bangor (6H) shed coasts over the hand operated level crossing and into the platform with an Up working. The fireman has prepared his fire in readiness for the departure after a brief halt. The single line tokens will be exchanged half way along the platform. The stone built office was solidly built and cosy, but the small windows allowed little illumination inside. There is a similarity between this structure and those on the Welsh Highland Railway constructed by the North Wales Narrow Gauge Railways on the northern section of the line. Notice the Down starter is the old wooden post lower quadrant LNWR design.   *J.H. Moss.*

Llangybi. n.d. Facilities at Llangybi were minimal and amounted to a signal cabin containing fifteen levers controlling points and signals. The single line token instruments were contained in the station office at the foot of the ramp to the Up platform. A small hut along the platform provided some shelter for passengers, but the Down platform was devoid of any such comfort. Passengers for Chwilog, Afonwen and beyond (such as there were) usually waited in the office until the train was at the platform and crossed the line on the level at the foot of the ramp. The Up line was on a rising gradient and a trap point was located at the foot of the ramp and can be seen by the walk way. Drivers drew the stock well clear of this potential hazard and sanded the rails as they drew to a halt. The platform edging were replaced in the early 1950s.
    W.G. Rear collection.

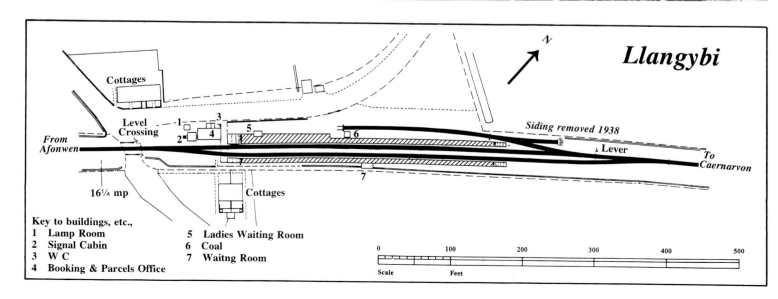

Llangybi

Cottages

Level Crossing

From Afonwen

16¼ mp

Cottages

Siding removed 1938

Lever

To Caernarvon

Key to buildings, etc.,
1 **Lamp Room**   5 **Ladies Waiting Room**
2 **Signal Cabin**   6 **Coal**
3 **W C**   7 **Waitng Room**
4 **Booking & Parcels Office**

Scale   Feet

0   100   200   300   400   500

Ynys. 5th May 1961. Despite its short length, Ynys seemed better provided for passenger comforts than Llangybi. The low platform height required portable steps to be on hand for alighting and boarding passengers. Behind the station name board can be seen the small six lever frame of which two were spare and the remainder controlled signals. The indicator instruments were located behind the frame protected by a wooden box. The first wooden building was the office and the waiting shed beyond that. Another small shed at the northern end of the platform plus a couple of lamp posts which held long burning oil lamps sufficed as furniture. Beyond the platform the line curves out of sight as the gradient eases slightly after the ungated occupation crossing.   *D. Thompson.*

Ynys. 1958. Looking south, the Station Master's house stood between the platform ramp and the level crossing. The gates were hand operated, and locked by a key. Beyond the crossing a permanent way hut stands on the Down side and the track curves away down the grade towards Llangybi. Apart from the staff house, the station was in an isolated position and a couple of houses nearby made up the community. Surprisingly the station remained open until the line closed, and rail services were replaced by a minibus operated by Crosville on Wednesdays and Saturdays to and from Pwllheli. This service lasted but a few years before it was withdrawn as uneconomic.   *J.H. Moss.*

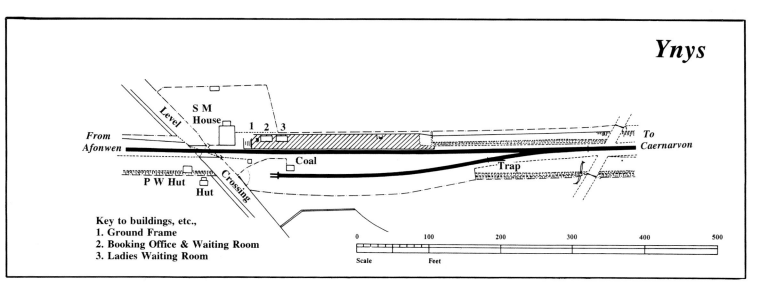

Ynys

S M House

1 2 3

From Afonwen

To Caernarvon

Level Crossing

Coal

Trap

P W Hut

Hut

Key to buildings, etc.,
1. Ground Frame
2. Booking Office & Waiting Room
3. Ladies Waiting Room

0   100   200   300   400   500

Scale   Feet

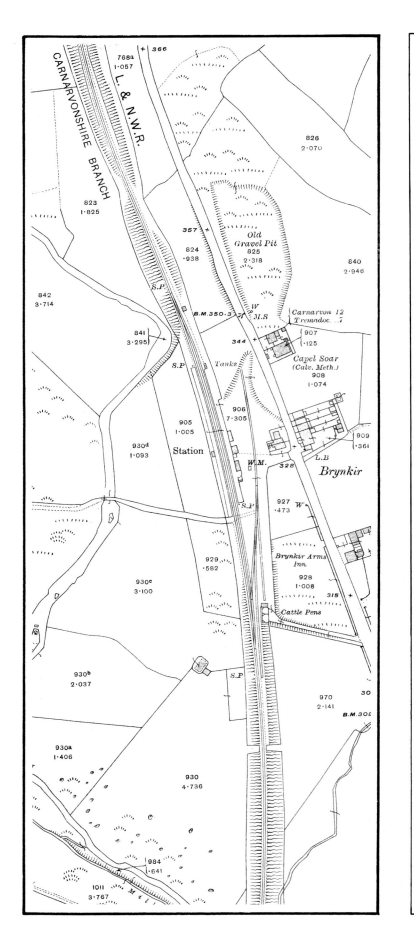

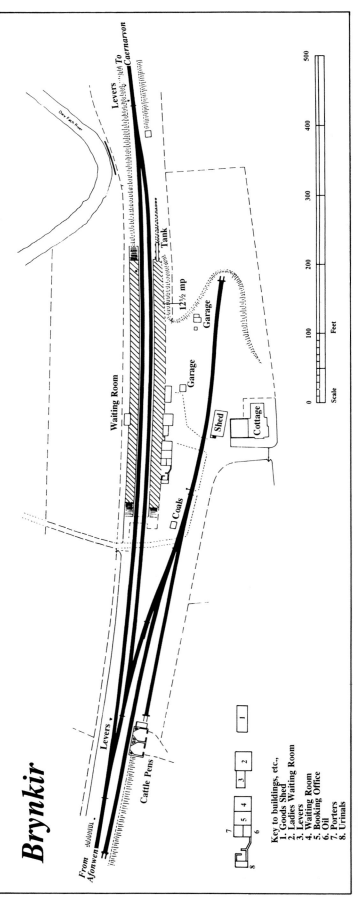

Brynkir

Key to buildings, etc.,
1. Goods Shed
2. Ladies Waiting Room
3. Levers
4. Waiting Room
5. Booking Office
6. Oil
7. Porters
8. Urinals

Brynkir. n.d. Brynkir station was another passing point on the single line, and an important weekly livestock market was held on land adjoining the station and which brought business to the railway. A small goods yard was located behind the main buildings on the Down side. This view shows these buildings on the low platform - a relic of the Carnarvonshire Railways - which necessitated portable steps being on hand to aid passengers. The water column on the Up platform, seen here with its attendant fire devil, was much in use, particularly on summer Saturdays when delays in running between passing points meant that trains could be held up for some time and it was deemed prudent to top up the tank on north bound trains. This entailed drawing up twice when traincrews of double headed workings both decided to play safe. The Up platform was built later than the Down side and constructed to a higher level, thus avoiding the necessity of portable steps.
British Railways L.M. Region.

Brynkir. n.d. Down trains coasted most of the way from the summit, and firemen took it easy after the unremitting slog from Caernarvon. Here British Railways Standard Class 4MT 2-6-4T No.**80090** of Bangor shed rolls to a halt at the Down platform. The porter signalman emerges from the station office bearing the long staff for the section to Llangybi. The main station building also served as the goods office. Illumination was by long burning oil lamps enclosed in cases, several of which can be seen mounted on posts or on the wall of the building.
W.A. Camwell.

Brynkir. 1960. Brynkir, in common with many other branch line stations in North Wales did not boast the luxury of having an enclosed signal cabin provided, but mounted the frame on a raised plinth on one of the platforms. There was little need for full time signalmen, so porter-signalmen were used instead. The frame at Brynkir was similar to that at Groeslon, located between buildings, and consisted of a standard LNWR design sixteen lever frame with stirrup release, controlling points and signals. Indicator instruments are mounted on posts, enclosed in boxes behind the frame. The single line token instruments were located in the station office. *J.H. Moss.*

Brynkir. n.d. On sunny days Brynkir station was a very pleasant place, and the staff were encouraged to develop flower beds to brighten up the platforms in their slack moments. The platform was host to the main building, constructed of brick, another brick building and a wooden shed which was used as a goods store. A cattle dock existed beyond the platform and there was regular livestock traffic until the late 1950's. A Camping Coach was installed in the cattle dock siding beyond the pens and despite the proximity of the livestock market, was very popular and frequented by regular holidaymakers who enjoyed the surrounding countryside and returned year after year. The Up platform shelter looks isolated but the platform staff kept it clean and tidy inside, with a good fire during the winter months. Some protection was given by thick box hedges grown especially for that purpose. *W.G. Rear. collection.*

Brynkir. n.d. Not all up trains took water at Brynkir but all drew well up the platform in case setting back was necessary. A trap point existed behind the photographer, and it is on record that at least one driver stopped his train short and suffered the indignity of having to call out the breakdown gang from Llandudno Junction. The surrounding countryside was bleak and the station was exposed to the elements. Passengers for Up trains were required to cross the line over the walkway at the south end of the platform and despite taking shelter in the booking office, usually got soaked by the time they boarded the train. There had been proposals to provide additional shelter in the early 1920's but this never materialised, possibly due to falling passenger receipts, accelerated by the regular bus service started by 'Busy Bee' buses that commenced operating between Portmadoc and Caernarvon in 1925. The bus concern was taken over by Crosville Motor Services in the same year, and three years later they commenced a service from Criccieth to Caernarvon which abstracted traffic even more. Despite the proximity of the station to the centre of the village, the bus service was even closer to homes and moreover delivered its passengers into the centres of Caernarvon and Portmadoc, which the railway could not. Nevertheless, traffic receipts were generally satisfactory until train services were withdrawn in December 1964. The author had the melancholy duty of driving the first rail replacement bus between Caernarvon station and Pwllheli via Glandwyfach on Monday December 7th 1964 when six passengers made the journey in the outward direction and ten boarded the bus on the return journey.
W.A. Camwell.

Pant Glas. n.d. This isolated halt near the summit of the line between Penygroes and Brynkir was located a quarter of a mile from the village of the same name. The development of bus services which passed through the village killed off most of the local passenger traffic. The station building has similarities with the Welsh Highland Railway buildings, already mentioned, both in the design of the structure and the use of yellow brick for window and door openings. The platform was of short length, and of low height, and freight traffic restricted to small parcels. At one time there was a siding on the Down side north of the level crossing gates but this was removed in 1947. The station closed to passenger services in 1957 but staff were on hand to open the level crossing gates until the line finally closed in 1964.

W.G. Rear collection.

Pant Glas. n.d. The reason for this staff group posing is uncertain, but probably they were involved in renovating and repainting the building and the level crossing gates and cleaning up the surrounding area of the station. Efforts to identify members of the group have failed, and any information would be welcome. It is believed that the photograph was taken by the late Oswald Jones, S. & T. Linesman based at Caernarvon. *W.G. Rear collection.*

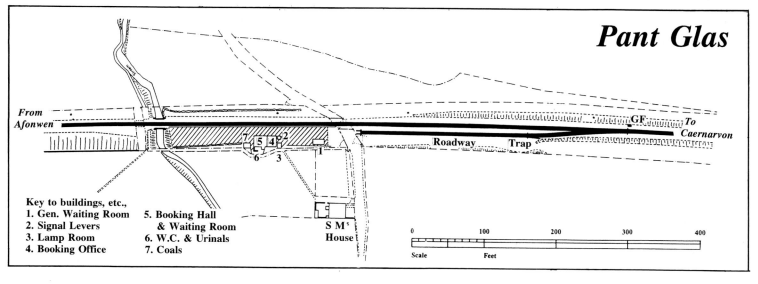

Pant Glas

From Afonwen

To Caernarvon

Roadway   Trap

GF

S Mˢ House

Key to buildings, etc.,
1. Gen. Waiting Room
2. Signal Levers
3. Lamp Room
4. Booking Office
5. Booking Hall & Waiting Room
6. W.C. & Urinals
7. Coals

Scale   Feet

0   100   200   300   400

Pant Glas. 8th August 1953. The ten coach Butlin's Specials were a feature of train working on the Afonwen line, mainly because the workings emanated from places in north west Lancashire, Yorkshire and Cheshire, and the train composition meant that locomotives were changed at Llandudno Junction or Bangor, the single passenger locomotive giving way to various permutations of standard LMS design tank engines, and crewed entirely by Bangor men. Here Driver Albert Victor Williams sits at the controls of Fairburn 2-6-4T No.**42157** piloting Stanier 2-6-2T No.**40102** of Llandudno Junction shed, with fireman Ieuan Williams taking a well earned breather as they approach the level crossing at Pant Glas with the W524 Relief to the 10.35am Relief from Liverpool Lime Street to Llandudno which worked through to Penychain. The Bangor men and locomotives took over at Llandudno Junction and after discharging their passengers at Penychain, worked the stock back empty to Llandudno Junction. Albert Victor had been on duty since 3.50am and had already worked one trip over to Afonwen and return with the same loco before he was requested to work this extra duty. By the time he booked off, he would have been on duty fifteen hours, not uncommon for Bangor men in the 1950's. *W.G. Rear.*

Grianog Crossing. 1966. The summit of the line was an exposed and windswept area, with little protection against the elements. A hundred yards towards Afonwen was a permanent way hut and two lengthmens' cottages in front of the occupation crossing which led to a small gravel pit. The crossing gates were normally across the road and the wife of one of the permanent way men received a small wage for opening the gates to road users when requested. This view is taken from the summit facing Pant Glas three months after the line's closure, and shows the state of things. To the right of the crossing is a spoil tip. The quarry worked sporadically over the years, but was acquired by a large consortium to supply gravel for use in the construction industry. At one stage in 1966 it was even suggested that the line be reopened to carry the stone away by rail. In the end the proposal came to nothing, and eventually the trackbed was utilised from Llanwnda to the level crossing shown here, as a private road for lorries only, working empty to the quarry. When the contract finished the trackbed was taken over by Gwynedd County Council and converted into a cycle path. *W.G. Rear.*

Penygroes. 11th July 1953. The climb out of Penygroes to the summit of the Afonwen line is demanding at all times, but none more so than that when the line capacity is stretched to its limits, with trains crossing at every passing loop between Caernarvon and Afonwen. As previously mentioned, most Summer Saturday specials to Butlin's Camp were double headed from Llandudno Junction or Bangor, worked exclusively by Bangor drivers and firemen. It was the normal practice for pairs of tank engines to work bunker to bunker, so that the leading engine was always facing the direction of travel, and any deviation from this policy met with disapproval by traincrews. Therefore this view is somewhat unusual but it must be confessed that it was pre-arranged between the author and J.M.Dunn, Locomotive Shedmaster at Bangor, who had long wanted such a photograph taking, that showed the tortuous climb out of Penygroes; he arranged it privately with the drivers concerned who were aware of the reason. So it was that Fairburn 2-6-4T No.**42156** piloted Stanier 2-6-4T No.**42628** on this one trip, with drivers G.O. Jones and W.H. Davies at the regulators. The train was the 8.15am SO. Manchester Exchange to Penychain due out of Penygroes about 12/01pm and running ten minutes behind a relief that had crawled up the bank in some distress. The departure from Penygroes had been explosive and despite the climb the train was still travelling about fifteen miles per hour as it passed the camera. Copies of the photograph were distributed to all concerned and JMD was delighted with the result. *W.G. Rear*

Penygroes. 30th August 1961. The Afonwen line was host to the passage of 'The Welshman', through coaches from Portmadoc and Pwllheli to Euston. The Up train is seen here entering Penygroes in the hands of Stanier Class 3 2-6-2T No.**40116**, which was drafted in for the summer season specially for this duty. There was a weight restriction over one of the bridges between Afonwen and Portmadoc which prevented the larger 2-6-4T locomotives from Bangor taking over the job, and the Stanier Class 3 engines were considered underpowered for the job. Be that is it may, this class of engine had a monopoly of the working from Portmadoc every summer since the end of W.W.II. The loco travelled L.E. from Bangor departing at 7.36am SX and reached Portmadoc at 10.20am after a wait of 55 minutes at Afonwen. It drew the three Class A coaches out of the sidings into the Down platform and topped up the tanks before departing at 11.00am, reaching Afonwen at 11.15am. Also at 11.00am Western Region men and loco from Pwllheli depot departed with three class A coaches for Afonwen, arriving there at 11.12am. These were then coupled to the stock from Portmadoc and the Class 3 departed with 6 coaches 201 tons at 11.27am. Caernarvon was reached at 12/13pm and the class 3 2-6-2T came off at Bangor at 12/36pm. In this view, the Nantlle Goods engine stands in the Down platform whilst a few passengers approach the train as it draws to a halt. *T.J. Edgington.*

Penygroes. 30th August 1961. Stanier Class 4 2-6-4T No.**42599** of Bangor (6H) shed pulls slowly alongside the Down platform with the thrice weekly goods for Nantlle, comprised of a box van and four mineral wagons. The slate traffic by rail had virtually ceased, what output coming from the quarries being transported by road. Notice the Up platform shelter, and the similarity of construction to the buildings at Pant Glas and those on the Welsh Highland. The station was always kept tidy and the staff won awards for the best kept gardens throughout the 1950's. The road overbridge beyond the footbridge still stands, with the inscription 'De Winton Foundry, Carnarvon' cast into the spans. The Down platform was also signalled for wrong line working, but instances of Up passenger trains using the Down platform are very rare.   *T.J. Edgington.*

Penygroes. n.d. The original station building was a solid depressing structure made out of red brick with traditional slate roof. The station master lived in part of the building whilst the rest served as booking office, waiting room, ladies waiting room, parcels office and porters room. There were some publicity boards mounted on the wall, but more information was supplied to passengers by the use of chalk boards as seen here. There was some protection for customers with the canopy extending part way over the platform, but this was ineffective for the last few yards dash to get into the coach.   *J.H. Moss.*

Penygroes. 1955. Four Fowler 2-6-4T locomotives arrived from Gourock in 1954 replacing four Fairburn engines of the same wheel arrangement. The parallel boiler engines were regarded as more powerful units than the ones they replaced, but the all enclosed cabs could become very oppressive in summer months, and the full height door made single line token exchanges difficult for the fireman. At Penygroes however, such exchanges were conducted whilst stationary, the signalman walking down from his box on the end of the Down platform to perform the duty. Here No. **42416** stands with the blower hard on, and visible signs of the fireman's preparations for the climb ahead. The three coaches are probably mostly empty and the bare trees and wisps of steam from the steam heating pipes indicate a winter period. A solitary wagon stands in the bay platform once used by the Nantlle branch trains. The photographer's camera case stands on the Up platform.

W.A. Camwell.

Penygroes. January 1948. A wintery aspect taken from the steps of the signal cabin and looking towards Caernarvon, with the photographer and signalman under seige from the porters. Three wagons stand in the former Nantlle branch platform, and the bare platform indicates a distinct shortage of passengers. The snow persisted and eventually the line became blocked by drifting snow at Pant Glas overnight. Fortunately no traffic was stranded, and after some digging out at Pant Glas and Llangybi, services were restored twenty four hours later.

W.G. Rear

Penygroes. 1958. Taken from the passenger footbridge and looking towards Afonwen, this view shows the southern end of the station. The small yard on the Up side was used to assemble mineral trains when the quarries in the Nantlle valley were in full production. Then the passenger branch engine, which worked the shuttle service to Nantlle, was used to ferry wagons to Penygroes to ease congestion in Nantlle yard. These would be uplifted by Up freight workings from Afonwen and conveyed to Caernarvon where they would be re-marshalled and worked forward to Mold Junction. The small coal siding had a steady business and received about three wagons twice a week. Behind the signal box, the Nantlle branch swings sharply left and commences climbing immediately to pass over the Caernarvon to Portmadoc road. There was additional siding capacity for wagons alongside the Nantlle branch and these were frequently full of empty wagons awaiting a trip to Nantlle. *J.H. Moss.*

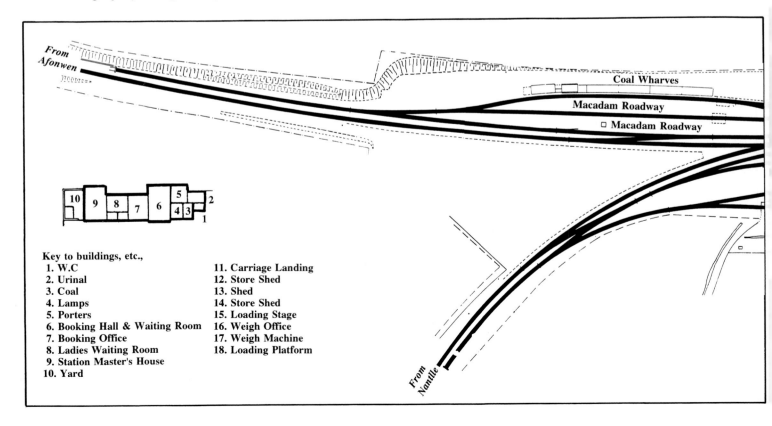

Key to buildings, etc.,
1. W.C
2. Urinal
3. Coal
4. Lamps
5. Porters
6. Booking Hall & Waiting Room
7. Booking Office
8. Ladies Waiting Room
9. Station Master's House
10. Yard

11. Carriage Landing
12. Store Shed
13. Shed
14. Store Shed
15. Loading Stage
16. Weigh Office
17. Weigh Machine
18. Loading Platform

Penygroes. 27th June 1956. Taken from the window of an Afonwen bound train, the starter has not yet been returned to danger. A mineral wagon peeps round the corner of the signalbox from its refuge in the Nantlle bay platform. Views of this platform face are very scarce. After the passenger service was discontinued on the Nantlle branch the line was used to load and offload materials from the adjoining raised bank which was constructed at the same time. The buffer stops were installed about this time as formerly the line connected with the bay line. Note the point rodding from the box to the trap points on the branch. Beyond the road overbridge stand the two starter signals. The Down line was signalled for two way working, but rarely invoked. *H.C. Casserley.*

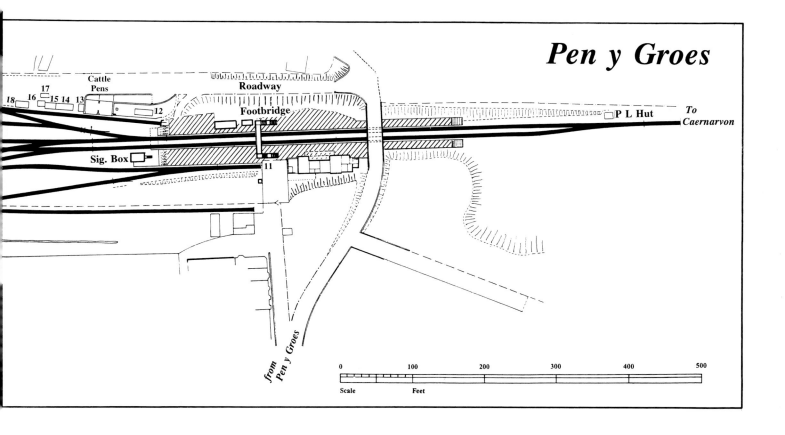

Pen y Groes

Cattle Pens
Roadway
18 16 17 15 14 13
12
Footbridge
P L Hut
To Caernarvon
Sig. Box
11
from Pen y Groes

0   100   200   300   400   500
Scale   Feet

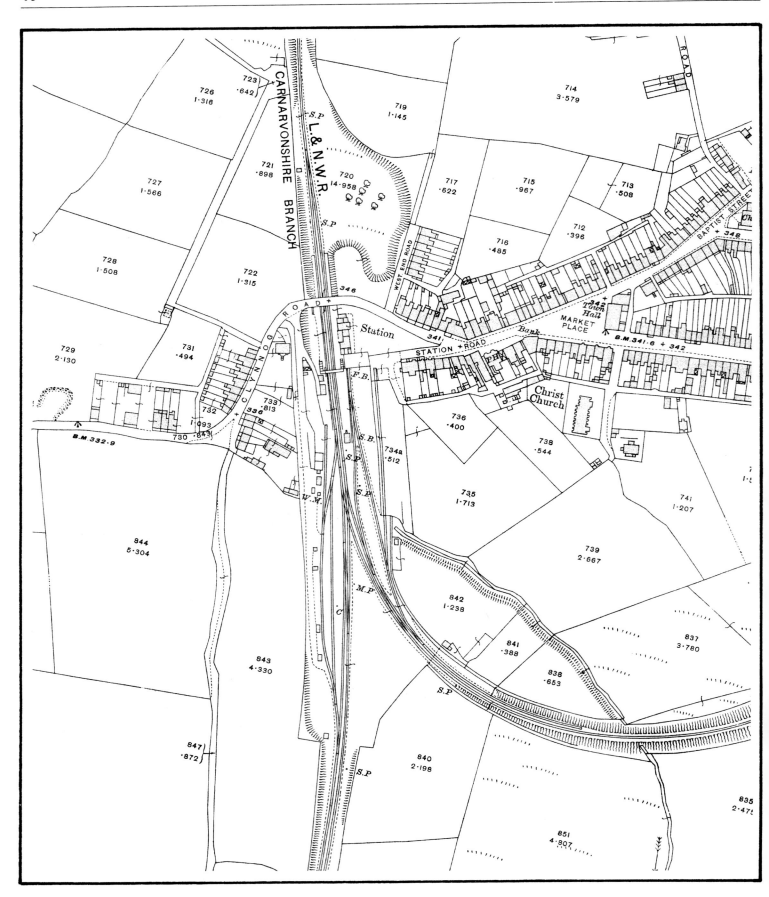

Penygroes-Nantlle branch. March 1952. At this date there was still a respectable quantity of slate worked down the branch to Penygroes, and small consignments of other traffic. Here Bangor shed's Stanier 2-6-4T No.**42460** waits with the Up 'Nantlle Goods' working for the road, which the author photographed from the footplate of the 12/20pm from Bangor to Afonwen. There was a bout of track renewal taking place on the branch at this time, and the materials were stacked alongside the line for much of its length. The signal wires for the two arm bracket signal run alongside the track, but the point rodding follows the siding line on the left. Notice the fixed distant for Tynyweirglodd level crossing. This was padlocked with the key attached to the wooden train staff, and the fireman was required to unlock and open the gates whilst the driver waited. After the train had passed over the crossing it was stopped again whilst the guard closed the gates across the tracks and locked them, and after indicating to the river that all was correct, the train would proceed the remaining mile to Nantlle. *W.G. Rear.*

Nantlle. 1955. Although passenger services were withdrawn from the Nantlle line on 8th August 1932, the passenger platform survived until the end. There had been some modifications over the years. When first opened for steam drawn passenger trains, a turntable was installed at the far end of the line, and engines turned as necessary. This had been removed early in this century. Beyond the station building stood a large water tank which survived in use until the line closed. In this photograph, the passenger platform can be seen together with the run round road. A mineral wagon stands on the tranship siding. *W.A. Camwell.*

Tanrallt Sidings. 1950. The branch to Nantlle was short in length and the road kept it company for most of the way. At one time a slate quarry had a siding on the Up side about half way, known as Tanrallt Sidings, but the quarry was worked out and the siding removed by the turn of the century. Speed was restricted to 10 mph but the time table was such that it was not necessary to reach this speed to complete the journey in the alloted time. In this view the check rail chairs have been replaced and stand out like new pennies on the old sleepers. In the centre distance stands the fixed distant for Up trains, protecting Tynyweirglodd crossing. The course of the line can be distinguished by following the buildings which kept the road company. *J.M. Dunn.*

Nantlle. 20th April 1957. For many years the motive power used on the branch was one of Bangor's two Fowler Class 4F 0-6-0. The volume of slate despatched at the turn of the century from the quarries was extensive as one would have expected and the goods yard was built accordingly. The decline in the slate industry during the depression of the 1930's affected the traffic shipped out of the yard, but even so there was sufficient traffic to warrant a daily train, until traffic was lost to road transport and the workings dwindled to three trains a week, alternating with the Llanberis goods. Once the engine had run round the train, the wagons were placed according to requirements, and since most of the traffic shipped out was slate, this meant that empty mineral wagons were placed along the tranship siding and loaded one moved away. These tranship sidings were raised above the level of standard gauge tracks and the slate, which came down from the quarries in narrow gauge (3ft 6ins) wagons, drawn by horse power, was run onto adjoining tracks and the slate transferred across the bank. In this view, Bangor's Class 4F 0-6-0 No.**44445** stands alongside the tranship siding whilst Nantlle Tramways horse *Dick* complete with a train of wagons stands alongside. Notice the elementary narrow gauge points.

Nantlle. 20th April 1957. The narrow gauge line entered the goods yard crossing the public road after negotiating the line from the quarries, which were owned by British Railways! Here a 'double header' return working to the quarry, with loaded slate wagons, this time loaded with coal. Access to the tranship sidings is clearly seen, but the quantity of standard gauge stock in the yard is misleading. Most of the vans were stored out of use and out of the way. In the distance behind the small black slate office can be seen the outline of the daily freight with its 4F 0-6-0 shunting the sidings.
W.A. Camwell.

Groeslon. 7th July 1960. No.75054 of Rhyl shed (6K) pulls away from Groeslon with *The Welsh Chieftain* Land Cruise train from Rhyl, bound for Barmouth via Caernarvon and Afonwen. The Standard Class 4MT 4-6-0's first came to Rhyl specifically for the two Land Cruise trains in 1957 and out of season wintered at Chester. They replaced Ivatt Class 2MT 2-6-0 engines from 1957 on, although the load and timings were only marginally increased. The original Land Cruise trains both worked in a clockwise direction, one starting from Llandudno and the from Rhyl whereas by 1958 one train worked in an anti-clockwise direction. The gradients were marginally stiffer anti-clockwise, which may be one of the reasons for using a more powerful locomotive.   *R.H. Short.*

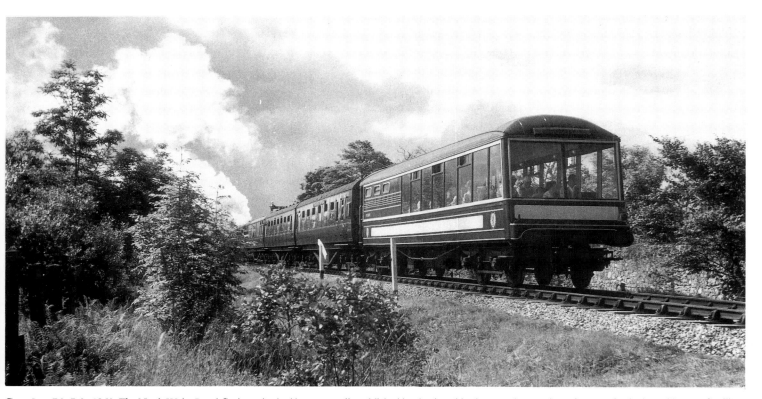

Groeslon. 7th July 1960. The North Wales Land Cruise trains had become well established by the time this photograph was taken, almost an institution with some families. For others, the car had intruded into their lives, and railway trips ceased to have the same attraction. Nevertheless the Chester District of the London Midland Region were innovative and replaced some of the older stock used on the Land Cruise trains in the early 1950's with more modern vehicles. In the formation of one of the two sets in use was this Observation Coach, formerly used on the Devon Belle, and which was used for a couple of seasons. For a small supplementary fare, passengers could watch the scenery unfold from the comfort of first class seating. Observation coaches were not new, and had been used on excursion trains to Blaenau Ffestiniog and Llanberis from LNWR days. Over the Afonwen amd Cambrian Coast lines, however, this was new ground. Sad to say the Land Cruise trains would only run for one more season before the powers-that-be withdrew them on the grounds of economy. Here *The Welsh Chieftain* pulls away from Goeslon on the leg to Penygroes. The gradient eases slightly from 1 in 61 to 1 in 75.   *R.H. Short.*

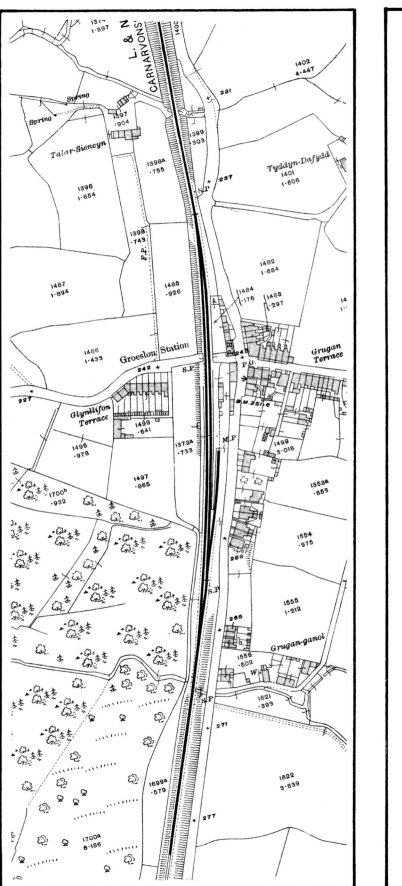

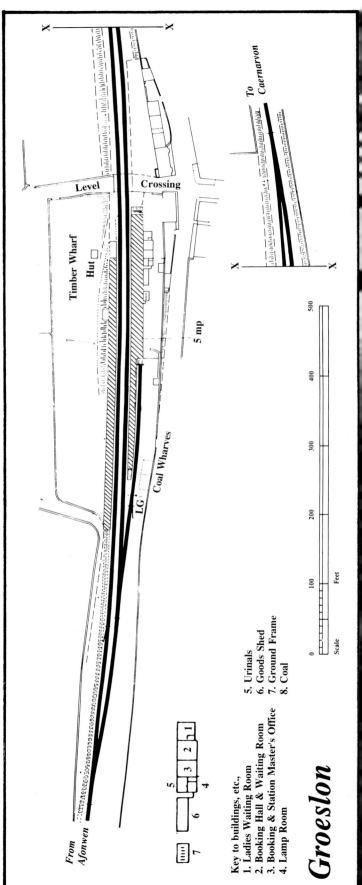

Key to buildings, etc.,

1. Ladies Waiting Room
2. Booking Hall & Waiting Room
3. Booking & Station Master's Office
4. Lamp Room
5. Urinals
6. Goods Shed
7. Ground Frame
8. Coal

Groeslon

Groeslon. 31st July 1958. Groeslon was another passing point between Dinas and Penygroes. The station was better patronised than most on the line, and was conveniently located in the centre of the village, and at a road junction with hillside villages. Here the photographer has taken a view from an Afonwen bound train of the departure from Groeslon, showing part of the extension to the Up platform. The train loco, No.**80090** of Bangor (6H) shed is at the head of the 8.25am Liverpool Lime Street to Pwllheli working and getting to grips with the task of getting the train in motion and the rising gradient.
H.B. Priestley.

Groeslon. July 1963. Fairburn 2-6-4T No.**42075** stands at the Down platform with the 1.30am Llandudno Junction to Pwllheli working which reverted to steam operation for the summer season. There is an air of neglect about the station. The loading gauge looks in a state of collapse, with one flap missing and the gauge held together with wire. Litter lies in the siding and the verges are uncut. In the distance, the guard has given the driver the green flag and in true Fairburn tank tradition, the injector blows back as the regulator is opened. *W.G. Rear.*

Groeslon. 1966. Taken after the line had closed and looking towards Caernarvon, this view shows the proximity of the station to the village. There was one siding off the Down loop, which was used by the local coal merchant who received wagon load consignments regularly and used the space alongside the siding to bag his coal direct from the wagon onto his lorry. Like many others in his position, when the line closed, he continued to use the site. *W.G. Rear*

Groeslon. 5th May 1961. The main station buildings were on the Down platform, whilst the Up side had a small shed to serve as a waiting room. Despite the fact that maroon totems were made for this and most of the stations on the line, Groeslon never erected them and the 'hawkseye' signs persisted until the end. The platform was of low height and portable steps were necessary to assist boarding and alighting passengers. A pair can be seen close to the platform edge awaiting their next call to duty. The Up platform was slightly higher, and passengers had to stretch! The hand operated level crossing gates were normally placed across the tracks and opened when trains were imminent. The Down line had received some new ballast which presents a very tidy appearance, unlike the siding which shows signs of neglect. *D. Thompson.*

Groeslon. 1963. In 1947 most of the passing station loop lines on the Afonwen branch were lengthened to enable ten coach trains to be worked to Butlin's Camp during the summer season. In Groeslon's case there was no room to extend south of the station so the extension had to be made north of the level crossing, which caused the inevitable build-up of traffic at times. Here a Saturdays Only ten coach train for Warrington straddles the level crossing awaiting the road to Dinas whilst the 1D11 - the 8.20am Manchester Exchange to Penychain enters the Down side and, as it is not booked to stop, will exchange single line tokens on the platform whilst trying to maintain momentum on the rising gradient. *W.G. Rear.*

Groeslon. 1964. The main station building at Groeslon was a small red brick construction on the Down platform, with yellow brick used to outline the corners of the structure, topped off with the inevitable slate roof. Beyond that a wooden goods store and beyond this was the open eighteen lever frame, similar to that at Bryncir. The platforms were extended in the 1920's, the extension on both lines made out of redundant sleepers. On the day this photograph was taken, an official tour of inspection was taking place to determine what assets were to be salvaged when the line closed. *W.G. Rear*

Llanwnda. 1st August 1958. Llanwnda station building was similar in appearance to Groeslon, namely a single storey structure built of red brick with cream brick corners and decorative lines running parallel to the platform. The station was situated on the edge of the village, but traffic never really developed and consequently some trains did not stop. In this view British Railways Standard Class 4 2-6-4T No.**80090** of Bangor shed draws to a halt by the platform with a Bangor working. The 'passengers' sitting on the seat are railway permanent way workers and their work has not yet finished. There was some spot sleeper replacement taking place and they were merely allowing the train to proceed unhindered. Once it has passed they will resume work.
H.B. Priestley.

Llanwnda. 1958. Another view of the station building, this time looking towards Caernarvon. The signal at the end of the platform is the Up Distant for Dinas just out of sight in the distance. At one time it was proposed to install a siding on the Down side of the line leading back to the road overbridge, together with a cattle dock & horse landing, but the scheme came to naught. Llanwnda station remained open until services were discontinued.
J.H. Moss.

Llanwnda. 1964. Probably the most profitable corner of Llanwnda station stemmed from this coal siding on the Up side. The local coal merchant received a couple of wagons a week which he unloaded and bagged in the yard before making his rounds. There was not much outward traffic and the small shed on the platform sufficed as a goods warehouse, although it was little used, most inward consignments being kept in the station office. The same tour of inspection was taking place as seen at Groeslon on the previous page, and it is significant that they travelled by road and not by rail. The road overbridge seen in the previous view was eventually demolished and the road level lowered, cutting off part of the goods yard in the process. A private road was made out of the trackbed from this point as far as Grianrhyd Crossing near the summit of the line to enable lorries engaged on construction works to by-pass Groeslon and Penygroes villages. After this traffic ceased the tarmacadamed trackbed was re-designated a cycle track.
W.G. Rear.

Llanwnda. 1964. Another view of the station building. and the wooden waiting room, taken at the same time as the previous photograph. The site has an air of neglect about it: the buildings and fencing are sorely in need of a coat of paint, the embankment on the Down side is uncut. Even the 'hawkseye' sign was never replaced although two replacement totems were made and remained in the office for several years before disappearing. *W.G. Rear.*

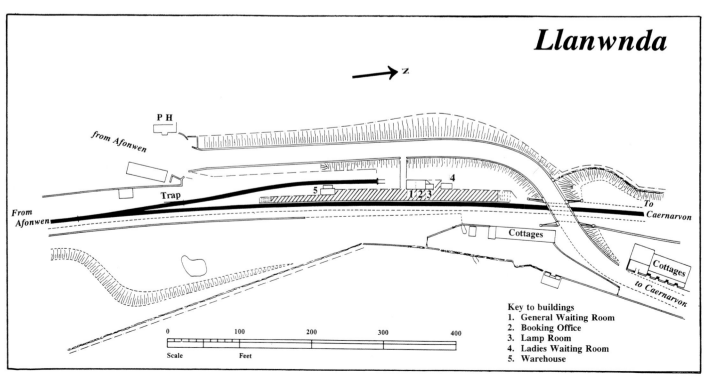

Llanwnda

from Afonwen

From Afonwen

To Caernarvon

Cottages

Cottages

to Caernarvon

Trap

PH

Key to buildings
1. General Waiting Room
2. Booking Office
3. Lamp Room
4. Ladies Waiting Room
5. Warehouse

0   100   200   300   400

Scale   Feet

Llanwnda. n.d. For many years Llanwnda station boasted a Station master, seen here resplendent in his uniform and smartly turned out complete with a buttonhole. It is believed that this gentleman was Mr Christmas Jones, but confirmation would be welcomed. He was regarded as quite a 'character' and several tales involving him, probably apocryphal, are told. *W.G. Rear collection*

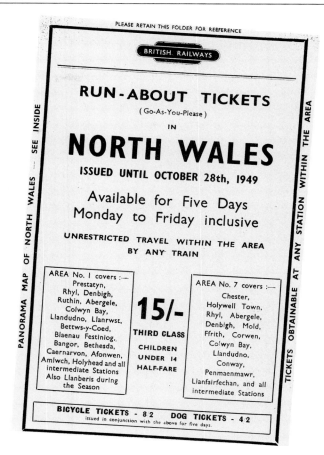

PLEASE RETAIN THIS FOLDER FOR REEFERENCE

BRITISH. RAILWAYS

PANORAMA MAP OF NORTH WALES — SEE INSIDE

RUN-ABOUT TICKETS
(Go-As-You-Please)
IN
NORTH WALES
ISSUED UNTIL OCTOBER 28th, 1949
Available for Five Days
Monday to Friday inclusive
UNRESTRICTED TRAVEL WITHIN THE AREA BY ANY TRAIN

TICKETS OBTAINABLE AT ANY STATION WITHIN THE AREA

AREA No. I covers :—
Prestatyn,
Rhyl, Denbigh,
Ruthin, Abergele,
Colwyn Bay,
Llandudno, Llanrwst,
Bettws-y-Coed,
Blaenau Festiniog,,
Bangor, Bethesda,
Caernarvon, Afonwen,
Amlwch, Holyhead and all
intermediate Stations
Also Llanberis during
the Season

15/-
THIRD CLASS
CHILDREN
UNDER 14
HALF-FARE

AREA No. 7 covers :—
Chester,
Holywell Town,
Rhyl, Abergele,
Denbigh, Mold,
Ffrith, Corwen,
Colwyn Bay,
Llandudno,
Conway,
Penmaenmawr,
Llanfairfechan, and all
intermediate Stations

BICYCLE TICKETS - 8 2   DOG TICKETS - 4 2
issued in conjunction with the above for five days.

Llanwnda. July 1952. The Ivatt Class 2 tender engines were rarely seen on the Afonwen branch, although the tank engine equivalent were A familiar sight. However in the early 1950's, during the summer season, two engines traversed the line daily in one direction only. These were Rhyl based engines working the North Wales Land Cruise trains, running under reporting numbers W662 and W663 respectively. Here No.**46435** rolls down the bank from Llanwnda towards Dinas with the Llandudno-Rhyl-Corwen-Barmouth-Afonwen-Llandudno Junction-Llandudno train. A relaying programme was planned for the following week end and pre cast concrete sleepers can be seen on the far side of the track, together with the replacement rail in the four foot. *W.G. Rear.*

Dinas. 1964. The run from Llanwnda to Dinas was short, and for Up direction trains, there was no need for steam to be used, the gradient ensuring that trains rolled freely. Here the track to Llanwnda is seen from the road overbridge at the south end of Dinas station. In the distance, as the track swings into view can be seen Glanrhyd level crossing. The former Welsh Highland Railway once occupied the site to the left of the track, now occupied by the Welsh Water Authority, and a modern garage occupies the same site as the former engine shed. Behind the garage, the spire of Glanrhyd chapel rises above the trees.   *W.G. Rear.*

Dinas. 30th July 1951. Taken from the Up platform looking towards Afonwen, Stanier 2-6-4T No.**2539** still in LMS livery and as yet not sporting the London Midland Region prefix before the number, coasts down the gradient and having been checked at the home signal, draws slowly into the Up loop with the 10.50am from Afonwen to Bangor. At this point in time the station was still open to passenger traffic although it was unlikely that anyone would get on or off here. Services were withdrawn on 10th September 1951 but the signalbox and passing loops remained in use until the line closed in 1964. The signalman can be seen sitting on the seat awaiting the arrival of the train with the train staff in his hand for the section to Caernarvon. On the Down platform the former Welsh Highland Railway building stands unchanged although the ground behind the platform was being overtaken with scrub growth.
H.B. Priestley.

Dinas. 30th July 1951. A short while after the passenger train shown in the previous picture had cleared the section to Caernarvon, the Up 'Nantlle' Goods was offered by the signalman at Groeslon, and accepted. Ten minutes later it rolled down the bank to be brought to a stand at the home signal, which was the normal practice for unfitted freight trains on this section of line. Once the arm had been raised, the driver rolled into the Up loop and brought his train to rest. There would then be a wait here until the 12/20pm from Bangor paused at the Down platform and after changing single line staff for token, and proceeded towards Llanwnda and Groeslon, the line would be clear for the freight to proceed towards Caernarvon. Here Stanier 2-6-4T No.42460 rolls slowly into the loop. Notice the oil lamp in the glass case attached to the WHR building wall.

H.B. Priestley.

Dinas. July 1952. Immediately south of the station Stanier 2-6-4T No.42588 driver by R.J. Williams, (known as Bob 'Joy'), and Fairburn 2-6-4T No.42260 driven by W.H. Davies get to grips with getting the ten coach relief train to the 8.15am Manchester Exchange to Peny-chain on the move again after stopping to cross an Up working. This train was in fact run in two parts, hence the 'B' after the reporting number, and the train was running about an hour late, having been held up all the way from Chester. The two Bangor men took over the working at Llandudno Junction and were delayed at every passing loop until they finally arrived at their destination. The passenger stock was a mixed bag of what could be had from the reserve of coaches in Red Bank sidings. The leading coach had a brake dragging, judging by the smell and noise as it passed the photographer.

W.G. Rear.

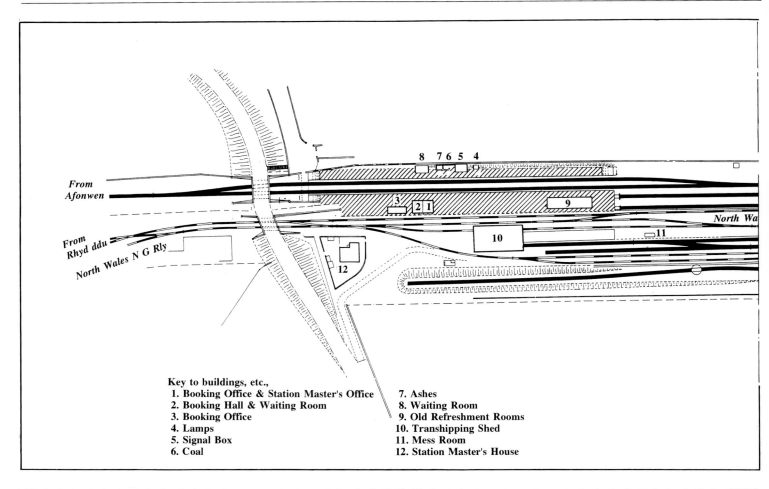

Key to buildings, etc.,

1. Booking Office & Station Master's Office
2. Booking Hall & Waiting Room
3. Booking Office
4. Lamps
5. Signal Box
6. Coal
7. Ashes
8. Waiting Room
9. Old Refreshment Rooms
10. Transhipping Shed
11. Mess Room
12. Station Master's House

Dinas Junction. c.1934. In pre-war days, when the Welsh Highland Railway was still running from Dinas to Portmadoc. Stock for the 1/30pm to Portmadoc stands on the narrow gauge tracks, each coach sporting a different colour in an attempt to boost trade. The large name board proclaims the destinations served by the WHR although trade seems very thin and the only passengers appear to be waiting for the next train to Afonwen. The WHR building appears in good condition and the growth between the two railways is kept low. There is little signs of life on the standard gauge line although a large crate stands outside the office and a pram is visible on the far corner of the building.   *Lens of Sutton.*

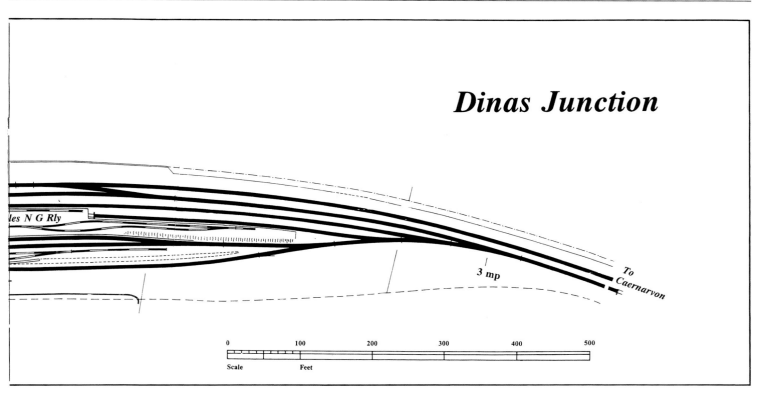

Dinas Junction

les N G Rly

3 mp

To Caernarvon

0   100   200   300   400   500

Scale   Feet

Dinas. July 1954. Bangor MPD Class 4 2-6-4T engines, Fowler No.**42416** piloting No.**42156** with the 9.40am SO. Penychain to Manchester Exchange pulls away from Dinas and onto the single line to Caernarvon. The loop commences by the third coach and was extended in 1947 from its previous position closer to the platforms. In the foreground can be seen the trackwork into the goods yard with the headshunt behind the camera. Although the yard was closed to freight traffic in September 1951 the trackwork remained, and it was used for some time as a crippled wagon store.   *W.G. Rear.*

Dinas Junction. 1936. The permanent way staff rarely featured in any photographs taken, and I am happy to redress the balance here. The resident ganger for the section between Dinas and Seiont Bridge on the outskirts of Caernarvon poses by the north end of the station. At one time the loop was much shorter, and access to the goods sidings on the Down side was via a lengthy headshunt. Entrance to the Down side loop was behind the camera. The lower quadrant home signal stands guard and alongside in the goods yard, a ground disc signal controls access from the yard to the main line.   *W.G. Rear collection.*

Llyn Padarn September 1952. The summer seasons before World War II saw regular excursions along the Llanberis branch from Rhyl and Llandudno, the formation of the train included an Observation Car. These were suspended for the duration of the war, and resumed in 1949 with one train running daily Tuesdays, Wednesdays and Thursdays at first, but in subsequent seasons, running from Mondays to Fridays inclusive. This working started from Prestatyn and returned in the evening to Rhyl. Before the war, Llandudno Junction men had worked one train, and Bangor men the other, but on resumption of the service, this was allocated to Bangor, to the exclusion of all other sheds, until the demolition of the line commenced, by which time Bangor shed was no more. In this view, Stanier 2-6-4T No.**42670** of Bangor shed approaches Llanberis tunnel with the 5/30pm seven coach return excursion. The lake is motionless in the still air, and in the distance the summit of Snowdon shimmers in the haze. This part of the trackbed is now a public footpath.   *W.G. Rear.*

Brynrefail. August 1952. Padarn Railway 0-6-0T *Amalthea* negotiates the level crossing over the Fachwen road with a train of narrow gauge empties bound for Gilfach Ddu, Llanberis, where the narrow gauge wagons would be off-loaded from the 4' 0½" gauge wagons. The level crossing gates were hand operated, the gate-keeper occupying the small hut in the left hand corner. The engines were equipped with chime whistle which could be heard three miles away on a still day. Across Llyn Padarn, British Railways line to Llanberis passes under the hillside. Cwm y Glo station is concealed by the house. Beyond the bridge over the mouth of the river Rhythallt, the two lines gradually converged and ran parallel for about two miles, eventually coming within fifteen yards of each other near Pontrhythallt. The 1' 10¾" gauge Llanberis Lake Railway was constructed on the Padarn Railway trackbed and has its northern terminus some twenty yards before the crossing.   *W.G. Rear.*

Seiont Bridge, Caernarvon. 1956. The former Carnarvonshire Railway met the Carnarvon & Llanberis Railway at this point and continued as two single but parallel lines almost to the foot of the castle, where they tunneled under Castle Square to make an end on junction with the London & North Western Railway at Caernarvon station. In this view, the Afonwen line continues to climb and swings out of sight into Coed Helen and the site of the former Pant station, the first terminus of the C.R. In the foreground, the Llanberis line falls away and follows the course of the river Seiont for most of its way to Llanberis.   *J.M. Dunn collection.*

Seiont Bridge, Caernarvon. September 1952. Taken from the Afonwen line and looking towards Llanberis, this view shows the stiff climb encountered by Caernarvon bound trains off the branch, enforced on the railway by it having to cross under the main Portmadoc road at river level before climbing to join the Afonwen line on the mile long run to Caernarvon station. Here No.**42617** working the 5/30pm Llanberis to Rhyl return excursion shuts off steam and coasts over the summit before descending to harbour level in front of the castle.   *W.G. Rear.*

Peblig Mill, Caernarvon. 1964. The Llanberis line at one time had siding connections with two brickworks on the outskirts of Caernarvon. The second works at Peblig ceased production before W.W.II and the siding was dormant for many years. During the war, however, a factory was built to produce armaments and the rail connection was revived for this purpose, although little use was made of the rail facility. The building was taken over by Bernard Wardle who developed a plastic fabric process and employed many people until it closed in the late 1970's. They had no use for the rail connection and it was taken out about 1950. The line is seen here passing the back of the Bernard Wardle factory before passing under the Caernarvon-Waunfawr-Beddgelert road in the distance.　　*W.G. Rear.*

Peblig Mill. August 1952. Stanier Class 4MT 2-6-4T No.**42460,** working excursion No.W635 Rhyl to Llanberis, heels over into the curve as it approaches the first of eight bridges over Afon Seiont. This working subsequently gained the status of a named train, rejoicing in the title *The Snowdonian* and which conveyed the LNWR built observation car in its formation. Sadly it never carried a smokebox nameplate, only carriage boards. The loco was a long time resident of Bangor and was regarded as a strong and good steaming engine. This working departed Rhyl at 9.30am and was worked throughout by Bangor No.2 Link men. The train was due in Llanberis about 11.20. Passengers were allowed sufficient time to ascend Snowdon by train before departing back to Rhyl.　　*W.G. Rear.*

Peblig Mill. June 1952. Stanier Class 4MT 2-6-4T No.**42617** coasts down the 1 in 62 having crossed Afon Seiont for the eighth time in three miles, and seen here approaching the bridge carrying the Beddgelert road over the line. The train was a Saturdays Excepted from Llanberis to Caernarvon after working the W635 from Rhyl to Llanberis. At Caernarvon the Bangor No.2 Link traincrews changed over. The locomen cleaned the fire and took on water prior to returning to Llanberis. It was unusual to find a two-coach articulated set working back with the engine, normally it was the observation coach that accompanied the loco. This particular working was not advertised, but made a good connection with an Afonwen to Bangor working, which in turn connected with a Holyhead to Crewe train and was well supported. On this particular day there were over fifty passengers booked from Llanberis which necessitated the use of the two-coach set.　　*W.G. Rear.*

Pontrhythallt. 1958. The intermediate stations between Caernarvon and Llanberis were similar in appearance, built of dressed granite with windows and door frames faced in brick. The platforms were of short length, which was satisfactory for short trains of six wheel passenger stock which worked the line until the mid 1920's, but not long enough for the more modern stock that replaced the original sets. The railway followed the course and crossed over Afon Seiont several times including here at the north end of the station. The bridge abutments were built wide enough to accommodate a wooden platform extension and the original platform extended over the river but this was cut back to 180ft in length after the Second World War. There was a small frame for six levers mounted on the platform controlling signals. Access to the goods yard on the Up side was by a pair of two-lever ground frames at each end of the loop, unlocked by the train staff for the Pontrhythallt to Llanberis section. The local coal merchant used the goods yard to stock his coal supplies which originally came in by rail, but after closure was delivered by heavy lorry. This view shows the station looking towards Llanberis, with Snowdon towering in the background. *J.H. Moss.*

Pontrhythallt. 3rd September 1964. This was the last goods train to work on the Llanberis line and comprised a GWR brake van, a covered van and a brake van. A panel of lap fencing was the final delivery to the station. The GWR brake van was included because the train carried an authorised passenger who had persuaded the powers that be of his need to travel by the last train. An inspector was briefed to accompany the gentleman, seen here supervising the proceedings. The loco was the usual 2-6-4T No.**42489** of Bangor shed. Demolition of the line started the following year, and recovery trains worked from Llandudno Junction. *E.N. Kneale.*

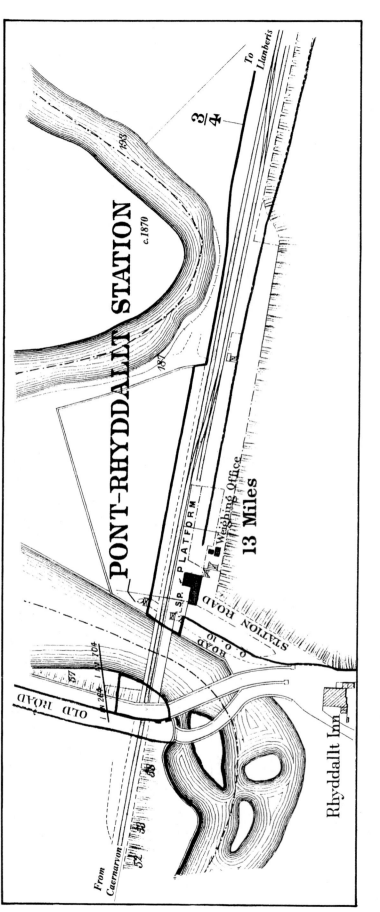

PONT-RHYDDALLT STATION c.1870

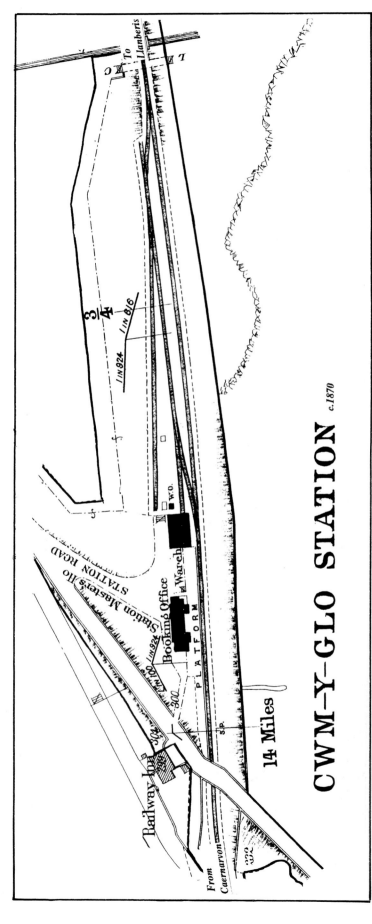

CWM-Y-GLO STATION c.1870

Cwm y Glo. 1957. The station at Cwm y Glo was hemmed in between the river and a rocky bluff, which made photography in the station somewhat difficult. The building was similar in appearance to that at Pontrhythallt and Llanberis. There was a Goods Shed located on the Down side and two sidings, one of which entered the shed. There was a certain amount of coal traffic delivered here which was distributed to the surrounding villages. After regular services ceased in 1930 excursion traffic still called at the station but this ceased in 1939 and never resumed afterwards, although some Sunday School excursions originating in the valley picked up and set down passengers in the early 1950's. *J.M. Dunn.*

Cwm y Glo. 1965. The line ran along the valley floor seen here from a rocky outcrop near Llanberis tunnel. The yard full of wagons is deceptive; these were parked for the demolition squad, who loaded them with recovered materials which was then carried away by a daily freight train which worked to the rail head every morning. The trackbed was subsequently used for a realigned road at this point. The goods shed and station were demolished in the late 1970's. *W.G. Rear.*

Cwm y Glo. 1965. The goods shed was rarely used to capacity, and most traffic transhipped inside was agricultural produce and grain. The LMS Country Lorry service called at the yard daily. The second siding was used for the local coal merchant. The line climbs gently for another quarter mile before entering the unlined Llanberis tunnel just visible behind the rocky outcrop on the upper left of the picture. *W.G. Rear.*

Cwm y Glo. July 1953. Stanier Class 4MT 2-6-4T No.**42617** from Bangor shed heads for the short Llanberis Tunnel about half a mile beyond Cwm y Glo station, with the daily excursion from Rhyl, Reporting Number W635. Drifting exhaust hides the observation car which made up the seven coach formation, and which was still in the LMS maroon livery. During the Dinorwic Quarrymen's Strike at the end of the last century, the rock outcrop in the centre of the picture provided a suitable dais for the Union leaders to address its members. Sixty years on, a plaque to commemorate the significance of the site was erected on the side of the original road. Typically the road was then superceded by a new one built on the formation of the trackbed and which by-passed the village of Cwm y Glo; only walkers following the old road discover the historical importance of the location.

W.G. Rear.

Llyn Padarn. September 1952. Although the summer excursion traffic to Llanberis drew attention to the natural attractions of the area, the line survived due to the level of freight traffic carried over the years. Until 1957 this train ran daily, but traffic declined and the service was reduced to three trips each week, the work alternating with the Nantlle branch trip. In this view Stanier 2-6-4T No.**42455** of Bangor shed heads back towards Caernarvon with the return working and crosses the causeway built to avoid the necessity of excavating a second tunnel through a spur jutting out into the lake. The train is approaching Llanberis tunnel and s about half way between Llanberis and Cwm y Glo.   *W.G. Rear.*

Llyn Padarn. September 1952. The summer season daily excursion from Rhyl to Llanberis passed through some of the most impressive scenery in North Wales. Here Stanier Class 4MT 2-6-4T No.**42460** from Bangor (6H) shed crosses the causeway after emerging from the short Llanberis tunnel. Steam has been shut off as the train costs the remaining mile to the terminus. On emerging from the tunnel the damper would be shut and the fire made up, hence the dark smoke. The loco would stand at the platform for some time prior to shunting the Observation Car to the opposite end. This particular day was overcast, not a breath of wind caused a ripple to disturb the surface of the lake. Across the water the 4' 0½" Padarn Railway track skirted the lake, threading through the clumps of trees that fringed the water edge. Today the narrow gauge Llanberis Lake Railway runs the length of the lake on the far bank whilst the standard gauge track is now a public footpath.   *W.G. Rear.*

Llanberis. 1955. The rail approach to Llanberis terminus was one of the most picturesque in Britain, the terminus itself nestling under the lee of Snowdon itself, and alongside Llyn Padarn. The line crossed a small stream before the station itself and before the main platform was reached, encountered the former ticket platform - a relic from LNWR days when some stations were 'open' and people could wander onto the platforms without the necessity of buying a platform ticket. Ticket platforms were also installed at Amlwch and Caernarvon, but these were removed in LMS days. At Llanberis, however, the platform survived, and was subsequently proved very useful when longer seven coach excursion trains took up all the existing platform space and, apart from a small section at the end of the original platform ramp and the steps leading to the ticket platform, needed the extra length for passengers in the rear coaches to disembark without the need to walk through the train to the front. Another feature for many years at Llanberis was the siting of two Camping Coaches. One was located in the horse landing dock at the far end of the platform, the other was installed off the run round loop, seen here. The track was also well kept and the permanent way gang regularly won prizes for the best kept length.   *W.G. Rear.*

Llanberis. 1957. The station building at Llanberis was built with the same dressed granite as was found at Cwm y Glo and Pontrhythallt. The building at Llanberis was larger, reflecting its greater importance. The platform had a canopy extending part way into the platform, which gave some measure of protection. The canopy supports were to an unusual design, but identical ones were to be found at Betws y Coed. Beyond the platform is the goods shed, and until 1939 a single road locomotive shed stood adjoining the water tank. Both the loco and goods sheds were constructed of the same dressed granite blocks as found in the station building. A camping coach can be seen in the horse landing. Access to the goods shed was off the centre road over a crossing. Locomotives running around their stock in the platform latterly used the centre road, but before the war this was used to park stock temporarily and so locomotives ran into the coal siding and back onto the centre and then the running road, before setting back on the stock.   *J.H. Moss.*

Llanberis. July 1957. Another view of the station taken from the end of the ticket platform and looking south towards the stops. The ticket platform commenced by the Up starter, although the engine attached to a seven coach train in the platform was past the starter by at least one coach length. The camping coach is on the coal siding road, but this in fact provided a second run round loop off the centre road as mentioned previously. The footbridge was provided to enable pedestrians to cross from Station Road to the shore of Llyn Padarn over the tracks. Today, the station building is a shop and cafe, and the canopy area has been extended and enclosed to give a display area. However the proprietors have retained the canopy supports and built them into the structure. The inside of the station building bears no resemblance to when it was a station, with its booking hall and waiting rooms. The trackbed now forms part of the Llanberis by-pass.   *J.H. Moss.*

Llanberis. July 1957. Taken from the centre of the platform looking towards Caernarvon, this view shows the footbridge over the track, and the loop using the coal siding and avoiding the centre road, although most engines running around stock after W.W.II were not hindered by stock parked here and used the centre road run round. Notice the loading gauge suspended from the footbridge, the square wooden seats and the gas lamp near the platform ramp.   *J.H. Moss*

Llanberis. July 1957. The station exterior seen from Station Road. The station Master lived on the premises at the left hand end of the building. The structure lost a lot of character when the dressed granite was painted over. At one time a small canopy extended over the booking hall door. Above the station roof can be seen part of the Dinorwig Quarry complex.   *J.H. Moss.*

Llanberis. May 1947. The road loading bay at Llanberis goods shed, seen from the yard entrance. In the foreground stands the Morris Commercial three-ton flat coal lorry belonging to the Llanberis Co-operative Society is parked, its daily round having been completed. Beyond the goods shed can be seen the passenger platform and the landing dock to the extreme left hand side. About the end of May Camping Coaches would be taken from their winter store and, after servicing and effecting any necessary minor repairs, worked to their destinations. Two such vehicles were based at Llanberis for the season, which were worked from Caernavon on the daily goods. One would be located in the Landing Dock, the other at the other end of the station off the centre release road.   *G.H. Platt.*

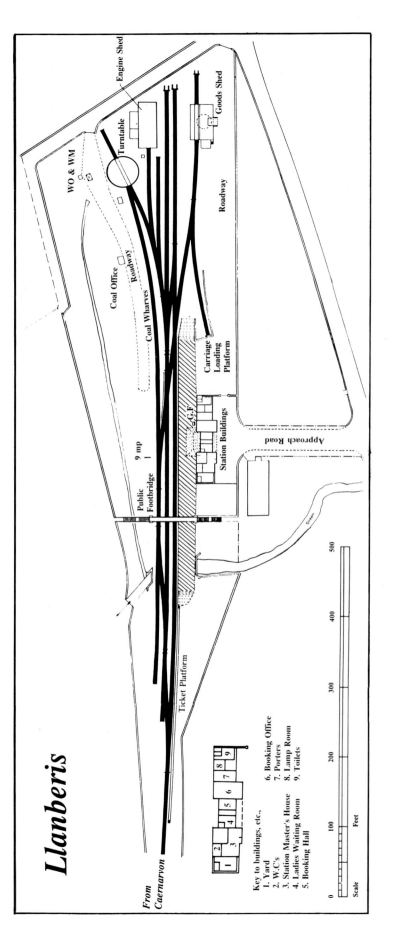

Llanberis

Engine Shed

Turntable

Goods Shed

WO & WM

Coal Office

Roadway

Coal Wharves

Roadway

Carriage Loading Platform

G.F.

Station Buildings

9 mp

Public Footbridge

Approach Road

Stream

Ticket Platform

From Caernarvon

Key to buildings, etc.,
1. Yard
2. W.C's
3. Station Master's House
4. Ladies Waiting Room
5. Booking Hall
6. Booking Office
7. Porters
8. Lamp Room
9. Toilets

Scale

Feet

0   100   200   300   400   500

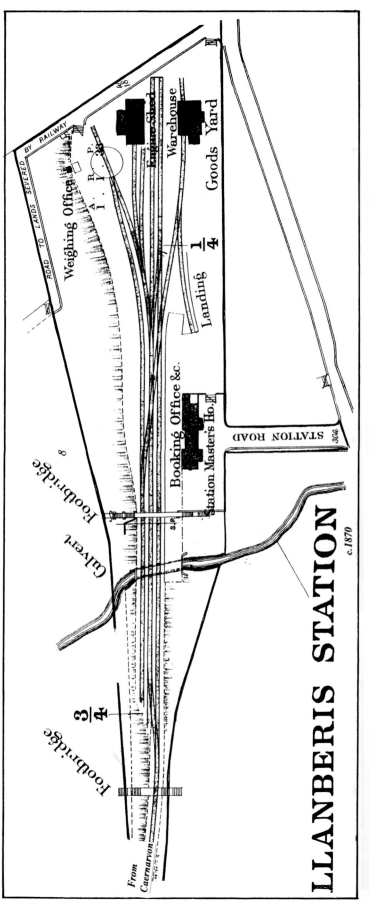

ROAD TO LANDS SEVERED BY RAILWAY

Weighing Office

R. P.
A. I.

Engine Shed

Warehouse

Goods Yard

1/4

Landing

Footbridge

Culvert

Booking Office &c.

Station Master's Ho.

STATION ROAD

S.P.

3/4

Footbridge

From Caernarvon

LLANBERIS STATION

c.1870

Llanberis. 20th October 1963. On this date the S.L.S. ran 'The Caernarvonshire Rail Tour' which visited the Bethesda and Nantlle as well as Llanberis. The locomotives used for the tour were Ivatt 2-6-2T Class 2 locomotives, Nos.**41200** and **41324**, both of Bangor shed, and specially cleaned up for the occasion. This view shows the special running into the platform road. Notice the station canopy support brackets and the three levers of the small five lever ground frame. The station is still very presentable, and it is sad to think that this was the last passenger train to use the station. *Brian Cowlishaw.*

Llanberis. September 1952. In the last week of operation Fairburn Class 4MT 2-6-4T No.**42260** stands at rest after working the Rhyl to Llanberis summer seasonal excursion (Reporting Number W635). In the foreground the Landing Dock stands devoid of the Camping Coach which was removed earlier in the week on the daily Class K freight. *W.G. Rear.*

Llanberis. July 1957. Much of the freight traffic that came to Llanberis was coal, and several coal merchants had their deliveries here. The largest of these was the Llanberis Co-operative Society, which shared deliveries with Deiniolen Co-operative Society. The coal was offloaded and graded in the yard and then bagged and weighed before being delivered to the customers in the respective villages. At one time the Deiniolen Co-operative Society owned three coal wagons, but details of these are unknown, the sole surviving evidence being a photograph, taken at Buxton, showing one of their wagons amongst others. The photograph is in the possession of the LMS Society. By the time of this photograph, most private owner wagons were a thing of the past, and coal was delivered to the same customers, but in B.R. owned mineral wagons. The siding curves round and ends at a 42ft turntable which originally came from Betws y Coed, but removed from there about the turn of the century. It remained in use at Llanberis until the engine shed closed in 1919, and survived until the line was demolished, although it had been out of use since the thirties. The engine shed was located and incorporated the surviving water tank, but that too was demolished in 1939. *J.H. Moss.*

Llanberis. 30th July 1948. Another view of the south end of the station, this time showing the side of the goods shed and flap plates in the horse landing. The daily excursion from Prestatyn stands in the platform road, with Stanier 2-6-4T No.**2462** at its head. In the coal siding, Fowler Class 4F 0-6-0 No.**4305** having placed another coal wagon in front of the unloading area, stands made up and ready to follow the tank engine back to Caernarvon once the former has cleared Pontrhythallt.   *H.B. Priestley.*

Llanberis. c.1932. Taken from the dead end looking north towards Caernarvon, this view shows the arrangement at the southern end of the station. The horse landing siding is taken off the goods shed road. The water column and fire devil stands outside the locomotive shed, not visible in this picture. Between the water column and the wooden coal office can just be made out the turntable release lever and handrails. *G.H. Platt.*

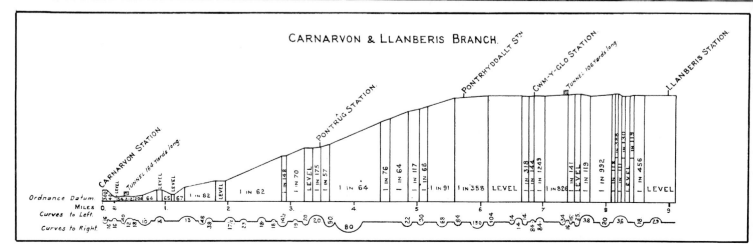

Caernarvon. August 1953. Two unknown Class 4 Tanks storm up the 1 in 64 from harbour level to Seiont Bridge, where the Afonwen and Llanberis lines parted company. This was an Saturdays Only extra working from Huddersfield to Penychain (Butlin's Camp) via Afonwen and the train consisted of a mixed bag of LMS stock of various vintages. The bridge in the foreground carried both lines over St.Helen's Road. It might be thought that the train was working 'wrong line' but in fact these were two single lines, the right hand track falling away just behind the camera constituting the Llanberis branch. The Permanent Way Gang were very proud of the standard of their work, having won the 'best length' of track competition for the district earlier in the year, which might account for the use of whitewash on the bridge and hut. Notice the flange greaser in the foreground, more for the benefit of Up trains heading towards Caernarvon, which encountered some tight curves in the next mile to the station.   *W.G. Rear.*

(*above*) **Caernarvon Harbour. 1965.** The climb from Caernarvon Harbour up to Seiont Bridge was fairly stiff, and the curves were severe enough to warrant check rails most of the way, which tended to give a musical accompaniment to the trip! The Llanberis branch and Afonwen line ran side by side as far as the bridge, but there was no physical link up between the two tracks after Caernarvon No.2 signal box. In 1965, after the two lines had closed to all traffic the demolition contract to lift the Llanberis line was awarded, and once more locomotives climbed the gradient on their melancholy journey. Demolition started at Llanberis and worked back. Until the railhead reached Pontrhythallt, the loco hauled empty wagons to that point, then leaving them in the goods loop, proceeded L.E. to the railhead, coupled up to the loaded wagons and returned back to Pontrhythallt where it left the loaded wagons on the main line and propelled the empties back to the rail head, with the brake van next to the engine. After detaching the empties, the engine and brake returned to Pontrhythallt once more, and before entering the goods loop, detached the brake van on the main line, ran through the loop, and set back onto the loaded wagons once more. After coupling up, the wagons were propelled up to the brake van, coupled up and made for Caernarvon. Once the railhead had cleared Pontrhythallt, the engine and brake van were propelled to the railhead from Caernarvon, first trip going up for loaded wagons, the second trip propelling empties. In this view, the brake van is being propelled towards Pontrug where the lifting was taking place.   *E.N. Kneale.*

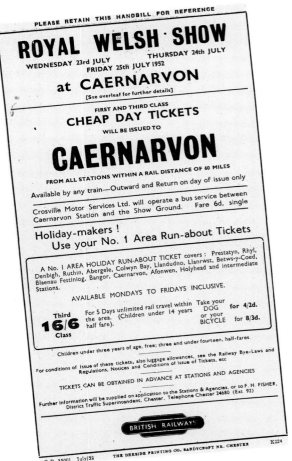

Caernarvon Harbour. September 1963. This view, taken from a footbridge over the line shows the two single lines looking towards Seiont Bridge. The two arm bracket signal with the Up Distant signals for Caenarvon No.2. signal box stand proud. Until freight traffic was withdrawn, there were usually a few vans or wagons to be found on the harbour lines. On the extreme right are part of the buildings that once belonged to the Engineering firm 'De Winton's', who made narrow gauge 'coffee pot' type vertical boiler quarry engines, and also cast beams for use on the Carnarvonshire and Festiniog Railways.

Caernarvon. 1965. The climb from Carnarvon tunnel was severe, with the curvature of the track adding to the problems of climbing the 1 in 81 gradient through the tunnel, which stiffened to 1 in 40 at this point, a quarter of a mile from Caernarvon No.2. signal box. Whenever possible enginemen were given the opportunity of taking a run at the bank, relying on the momentum to carry the train to the station. At one time the two sets of signals were located nearer No.2. signal box, but were replaced in 1947 and moved 300 yards down toward the harbour. It was at this point on Investiture Day, 1969 that a Class 47 Diesel failed to get a grip on the damp rails, and had to be 'rescued' by another class 47 sent down to extricate the victim. A nest of hard hatted inspectors appeared from nowhere and shouted instruction and counter instruction to the hapless Crewe driver without success. Eventually the relief loco arrived and pulled the culprit and stock back up the gradient and into the platform, much to the relief of the inspectors, who returned to their hiding place. Notice the route indicators alongside each signal.

W.G. Rear

Caernarvon Harbour. n.d. A fine panoramic view taken from the castle walls showing the course of the railway lines following the contour of the harbour. This view probably dates back to the 1930's judging by the variety of materials stocked on the waterfront. The upper reaches of the harbour have not yet been developed although the remains of old sailing ships that once rotted on the far bank of the estuary have disappeared. Eight wagons stand in the short siding by Carnarvon tunnel, which burrows under Castle Square before climbing up to the station. *G.K. Fox collection.*

Caernarvon. July 1952. The western approach to Caernarvon from the tunnel climbed at 1 in 40 for the last quarter mile, and after passing under a road overbridge alongside between the Red Garage and Crosville Motor Services' depot, the two single lines accessed the platform or goods roads through a scissors crossover. At one time an impressive signal gantry straddled the two lines but this was removed and replaced with the signals seen in the previous view. Goods sidings and the shed were alongside the Afonwen line. To the right of the Llanberis line is the back of the Crosville garage. During the summer months, the engine and observation coach off the Prestatyn to Llanberis excursion worked back to Caernarvon in order to perform loco duties and to change over traincrews. On arrival from Llanberis the train worked into the local platform and after taking water ran round the coach and drew out onto the Llanberis line before setting back into the Llanberis bay. The fresh crew travelled on the footplate from Bangor on the 2/15pm L.E. which returned to shunt Caernarvon yard and after stacking their personal kit had time for a brew before departure back to Llanberis. Here No.**42260** with the observation coach pulls out of the Llanberis bay platform. In the goods yard No.**41223** sets back onto a raft of wagons. *W.G. Rear.*

Caernarvon. November 1952. Stanier 2-6-4T No.**42617** rolls up the last few yards of 1 in 40 with the 10.50am Afonwen to Bangor working. The fireman will have crossed to the driver's side of the footplate ready to give up the single line train staff to the signalman in No.2. box, who will be standing in the six foot waiting to receive it. The No.1. goods siding is somewhat depleted of wagons, but no doubt will fill up shortly. Notice the water column and wooden post starter for the Llanberis bay. *W.G. Rear.*

Caernarvon. November 1952. W.H. Davies from Bangor No.1. Link leans out of his window as he drives Fairburn 2-6-4T No.**42259** out of the Up and Down platform at Caernarvon and negotiates the scissors crossover onto the single line to Dinas and Afonwen. The train is the 12/20pm from Bangor. Steam has already been shut off for the descent through the back of the town to the tunnel and out onto the harbour, where the continuous climb to Pant Glas commences. The fireman has built his fire up in readiness as the grey smoke indicates, whilst the safety valves lift. In front of the goods shed wagon loads of timber wait to be unloaded. Notice the wooden extension to the brick built goods shed. It was intended to be a temporary structure in 1910 but survived until the line closed. *W.G. Rear.*

Caernarvon. February 1953. Nestling under the shadow of Christ Church, Caernarvon No.2. signal box controls the Llanberis and Afonwen lines and stands at the ramp of the Up and Down platform. A standard LNWR design box, it contained a set of 51 levers. It was a very light and airy box, no doubt because it had two sets of windows in the back wall in order to observe movement in Llanberis bay line. The photograph was taken from the island platform, with the left hand face, known as the 'Local' platform, signalled for Up and Down line working. The right hand face was the Up line. The Local line starting signals and posts were replaced in 1951 but those on the Up and Down main platform retained the square wooden posts but had replacement upper quadrant arms. Just vsible under the platform canopy are the railway stables, used for horse drawn traffic until the late 1940's when the animals were replaced by motor vehicles under the LMS 'Country Lorries' service. *W.G. Rear.*

Caernarvon. 28th July 1950. Stanier 2-6-4T No.**42588** stands in the Local line of the island platform. This was a somewhat unusual occurrence, most trains to Afonwen using the main Up and Down platform whilst through trains to Bangor used the Up face of the island platform. Notice the covered footbridge which provided shelter for the passengers. When the island platform was modernised in the mid 1950's this covering was removed at the same time that the passenger shelter was rebuilt. This photograph was taken from the steps of No.2. signal box. On the right hand side can be seen the buffer stops in the bay platform, used by local trains to Llanberis until the regular service was discontinued. Before W.W.II, some excursion trains worked a shuttle service to Llanberis and made use of this platform. After the war, the locomotive and observation coach of the W635 excursion train from Prestatyn were worked back to Caernarvon about mid day to enable traincrews to be changed. The observation coach and loco were stabled there. The return working to Llanberis could then depart without a conflicting movement across the junction. *H.B. Priestley.*

Caernarvon. November 1952. Stanier 2-6-4T No.**42628** of Bangor shed draws away from the Up and Down platform and takes the right hand line to Afonwen with the 2/52pm from Bangor. The three coach non-corridor stock was unusual on this working, the return journey worked forward to Llandudno Junction and normally corridor stock was used. On the right hand edge of the picture can be seen the stables that adjoined the site. These had been little used since the mid 1930's, but during the early days of the war when petrol was scarce, a horse drawn dray was used on local deliveries, and a railway horse was resident. His reign did not last long and he was replaced by a motor lorry in 1945. The stables then stood unoccupied until the line closed, the buildings were demolished in the 1970's.
W.G. Rear

Caernarvon. 1941. In common with most stations, the staff who had not been mobilised were banded into a local Home Guard unit. The group is seen here posed on the Up and Down platform. The North Wales area did not suffer greatly during the war and apart from a few scares, time was spent on routine drill. Details of the functions of this group have not come to light and it would be interesting to discover anything about the men. This photograph is believed to have been taken by the linesman Oswald Jones.
W.G. Rear collection.

Caernarvon. June 1952. The original station building was enlarged shortly before 1911 when this brick booking hall was added to the original structure. The overall canopy was included at the same time. The booking hall itself had two ticket windows but some time before 1938 a gondola ticket office was installed inside the booking hall, and this was used until the line closed to Afonwen. Latterly the tickets were issued on the train by the conductor-guards. Passengers terminating their journey at Caernarvon usually had their tickets collected at a kiosk on the platform and passengers passed through the sliding gates and into the car park area. It was the practice for local taxi firms to meet the trains and there was great competition to tout for fares. Most of them were local and within the town, but occasionally one struck lucky and got a fare to the outlying villages. Some of the taxis were not licensed and there were several 'cowboy' operators, who used private cars and deprived the established operators of trade.
British Railways L.M. Region.

Caernarvon. 1965. The advent of the DMU brought some changes to the management of the station, particularly after the Afonwen line closed. However one of the long established traditions persisted for a few more years, none more so than the transport of the Royal Mail by train. Here the mail is being transferred from van into the care of the guard. Formerly the mail would have been handed over at each of the local stations on the line, but now it became necessary to bring it down to Caernarvon. The DMU will work the 16.55 to Llandudno Junction where the mail will be transferred to a Chester working. In the past, the GPO van would have not been allowed on the platform, the bags would have been loaded onto a barrow and a porter take them to the train. Now the reduction or absence of platform staff at all but the most important stations, meant that the postmen had to do their own unloading and it was considered safer to take the van as near to the train as possible. Another indication of the times can be seen in a suspended enamel sign at the foot of the stairs which reads "WAY OUT and BUSES FOR BUTLIN'S CAMP".
British Railways L.M. Region.

Caernarvon. c.1955. The station forecourt was a spacious affair, with plenty of space for cars to discharge passengers who could then walk under protection to which ever platform they wanted. This view shows the extent of canopy, from the Parcels Office along the front of the old building, into the Booking Hall, through the ticket barrier and over the footbridge. With the increase in cars using the forecourt, particularly the taxis, B.R. erected a protective barrier out of rail to protect its customers and property, after one or two encounters with vehicles failing to stop, and hitting the front of the building. When the Afonwen line closed, and Butlin's Camp passengers needed transferring to road, there was sufficient space to accommodate the buses necessary. In the first summer season this was undertaken, it was not uncommon to have twenty double decker buses in the yard at one time - a wonderful recipe for chaos. Butlin's Camp passengers took a dim view of the procedure, and the following season saw the number of passengers travelling by rail almost halved.   *L.& G.R.P. No.26682.*

Caernarvon. 1957. An interesting view under the canopy on the Up and Down platform looking towards Bangor. Notice the plethora of enamel signs - a collector's dream - not to mention the numerous totems suspended from the roof beams. In the foreground at the foot of the steps is the small ticket collector's office with the sliding door to the station forecourt hidden, although the shaft of sunlight betrays its presence. A barrow of mailbags stand unattended awaiting the next train. Beyond that are the twin pillars that indicate the entrance to the booking hall. Beyond the booking hall is the front of the old station buildings. Two barrows wait in the entrance to the porter's room, one carrying fibre tubs labelled 'Eldorado Ice Cream' and 'Lyons Ice Cream'. The second barrow is loaded with sundry parcels and packages. A pram stands outside the station master's window. The clock is motionless at five past two. Notice how clean and tidy the station platform is. The staff took a pride in their work, the station master was regarded as a person of authority by his staff and by the community in general. He would not tolerate a dirty station

British Railways L.M. Region.

Caernarvon. 1965. The 1950's saw many changes to Caernarvon station, not the least being the replacement of the buildings on the Island platform which were of wooden construction, and in poor condition, with a smaller brick shelter. A canopy of sorts was provided but it was a poor substitute. At the same time that these 'improvements' were being carried out, the covering over the footbridge was removed, making a journey to the Up platform an unpleasant experience in cold and wet weather, exposed as it was to the wind blowing off Caernarvon Bay and across the Menai Straits. During summer months it was not so noticable but warm days were relatively few in number and it was another factor that drove passengers off the railways.
British Railways L.M. Region.

Caernarvon. July 1965. Another view of a summer Saturday on Caernarvon station after the Afonwen line closed. An unrecorded Class 5 stands at platform 1 with the 11.20am Caernarvon to Manchester. In the Local platform, a DMU for Llandudno Junction stands awaiting its time whilst the Up and Down platform is roped off to contain passengers waiting for a relief to Liverpool Lime Street that was running late. Notice the double flow water tank, which was frequently drained dry in earlier days by two trains filling up the tanks simultaneously.
E.N. Kneale.

Caernarvon. 1960. The station exterior was somewhat unimpressive, and was inhibited by additions to the structure over the years. The Booking Hall, built in 1911 stands at the far end with the railings to the Parcels Office jutting out into the roadway. Beyond that a small outbuilding for the Station master's use. Access to Station House was through the gate and up steps to the first floor and the residential part of the building. By all accounts the living quarters were draughty and required big fires most days. The small wooden gate in the centre of the picture led to the excursion platform, which was opposite the Bangor Bay, and rarely used. It was built for the Investiture of the Prince of Wales in 1911. At the time of that Investiture another footbridge was built with an access from the roadway across to the Island Platform, but this was removed after a short while. On photographs taken about 1924 there is no trace to be seen of it. In the far distance, under the shadow of Christ Church can be seen the former stables. *G.H. Platt.*

Caernarvon. 1965. Whilst it is admitted that the overall canopy made the interior of the Booking Hall dull and poorly lit, the removal and subsequent rendering of the extension building in a red paint tended to make the building look even worse. This view shows the effect which was bad enough when the paint was new, but after a couple of years when it had weathered and started to flake, it degenerated to look downright seedy. This view was taken shortly after the painting.
British Railways L.M. Region.

Caernarvon. 1957. Another view of the Up and Down platform looking towards Afonwen. The extent of the canopy over the platform and footbridge can be seen from this view, showing the protection offered to passengers. The same extensive display of enamel signs is shown to good effect. Notice the ticket collector's office beyond the booking hall. Notice too the postal letter box on the side of the wall, with the train on line indicator above it. Another barrow with fibre 'Lyons Ice Cream' boxes awaits the next train. Beyond the footbridge can be seen part of No.2. signal box, with the Llanberis bay platform alongside. This part of the bay extended beyond the signal box. *British Railways L.M. Region.*

Caernarvon. 5th May 1957. The main platform at Caernarvon was signalled for bi-directional working, and was known locally as the 'Up & Down' platform, which could comfortably accommodate a fifteen coach train. The line extended beyond the platform and continued as the single line from Caernarvon No.2 box to Llanberis. The island platform in the centre of the picture was installed during the enlargement of the station at the turn of the century. The left hand platform was known as the 'Local' line, and was also bi-directional, but not used for passenger work on a daily basis. The opposite face was the main Up platform line, and to the right of this was the Up Goods Line and as such was signalled for through running. The bay line and platform to the left of the Up and Down platform was known as the Bangor bay, and in regular use until 1964. Stock off the last Down arrival from Bangor was stored overnight and which formed the first Up departure next morning. There was another bay platform alongside, known as the Excursion platform, but not used for passenger use after 1939. *Author's collection.*

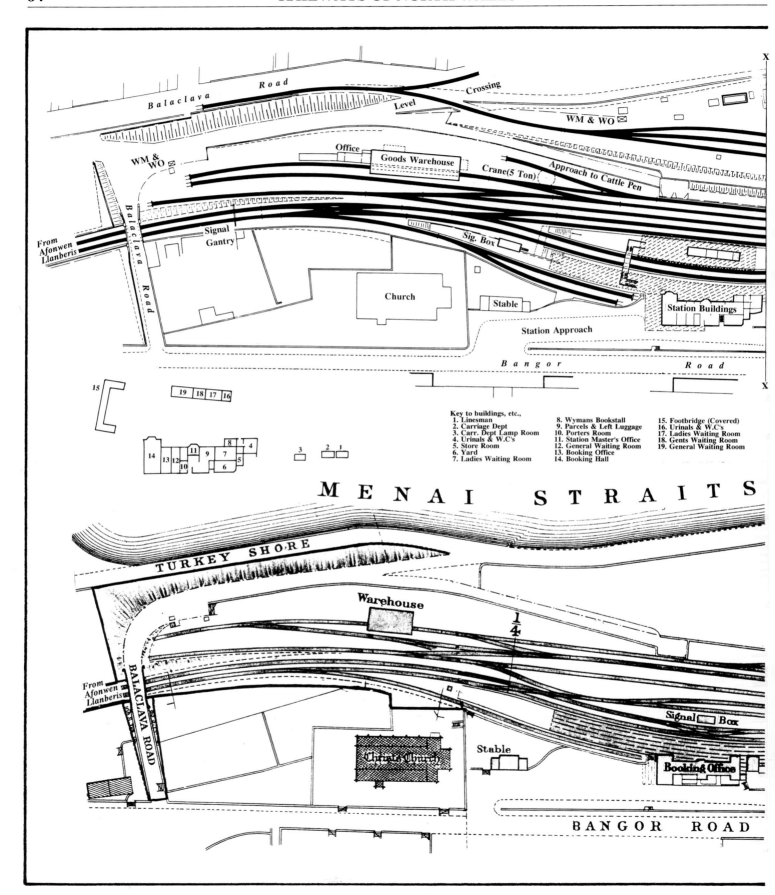

Balaclava   Road

Level   Crossing

WM & WO

WM &
WO

Office   Goods Warehouse

Crane(5 Ton)   Approach to Cattle Pen

From
Afonwen
Llanberis

Signal
Gantry

Sig. Box

Church

Stable   Station Buildings

Balaclava   Road

Station Approach

Bangor   Road

X

15   19 18 17 16

Key to buildings, etc.,
1. Linesman
2. Carriage Dept
3. Carr. Dept Lamp Room
4. Urinals & W.C's
5. Store Room
6. Yard
7. Ladies Waiting Room
8. Wymans Bookstall
9. Parcels & Left Luggage
10. Porters Room
11. Station Master's Office
12. General Waiting Room
13. Booking Office
14. Booking Hall
15. Footbridge (Covered)
16. Urinals & W.C's
17. Ladies Waiting Room
18. Gents Waiting Room
19. General Waiting Room

14 13 12 11 9 7 8 4 5   3 2 1
10 6

M E N A I   S T R A I T S

TURKEY SHORE

Warehouse   ¼

From
Afonwen
Llanberis

BALACLAVA ROAD

Christ Church

Stable   Signal Box

Booking Office

BANGOR   ROAD

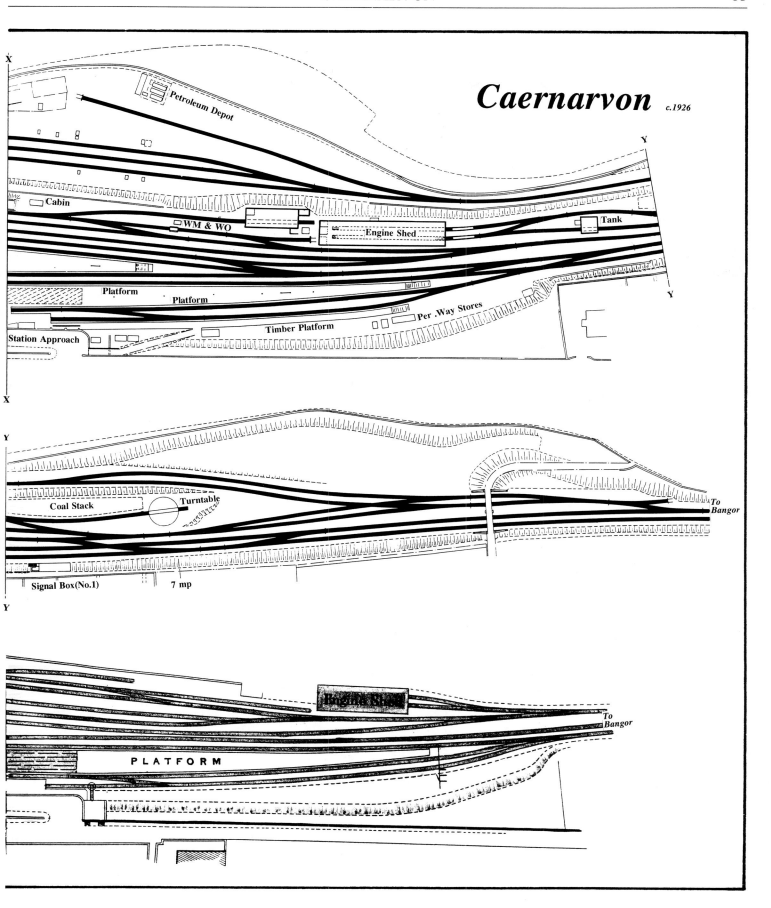

Caernarvon *c.1926*

Petroleum Depot

Cabin

WM & WO

Engine Shed

Tank

Platform

Platform

Per .Way Stores

Timber Platform

Station Approach

Coal Stack

Turntable

To Bangor

Signal Box(No.1)

7 mp

Engine Shed

To Bangor

P L A T F O R M

Caernarvon. June 1965. As if to emphasise the numbers of passengers travelling by train on a summer Saturday, this view was taken of passengers waiting for the 11.20am Caernarvon to Manchester train which seemed near to saturation. When the train arrived, it carried six hundred people for Butlins Camp, who were trying to get off the train and up the stairs whilst the crowd seen here were trying to get on the train. Chaos reigned supreme, but not before some angry words were exchanged and at least two sets of luggage never left the train and went back to Manchester. As the summer season reached its peak, things grew steadily worse, but people didn't forget and the following season saw many fewer people travelling.
W.G. Rear

Caernarvon. 4th May 1963. Sir Billy Butlin purchased several locomotives which were installed in his various holiday camps. Stanier Pacific N0.**6203** *Princess Margaret Rose* was placed on display at Pwllheli, and in May 1963 after a repaint in Crewe Works was drawn by Ivatt Class 4 2-6-0 No.**43052** of Crewe, to Penychain, via Llandudno Junction and Caernarvon and then over the Afonwen line. The convoy is seen here pulling out of Caernarvon Up and Down platform on the final leg of the journey, having got the single line token and received the signal.
E.N. Kneale.

Caernarvon. July 1964. The last summer of the Afonwen line saw the usual abundance of steam on summer Saturdays when most workings to and from the camp were double headed. There was one interesting variation from previous years, in that more workings over the branch involved Class 5 4-6-0 locomotives, which nevertheless required piloting from and to Caernarvon. In some cases the pilot engine was detached at Caernarvon and held over to await the next Down train. In this view, the working is the 10.45am Portmadoc to Manchester, Reporting Number 1C77. B.R. Standard Class 3 No.**82032** brought the four coach train to Caernarvon, where it unhooked and moved clear. An unidentified Class 5 4-6-0 then set back on the stock with another seven coaches and 82032 then attached on front as pilot as far as Bangor. A 2-6-4T stands in the Bangor bay after piloting the 10.40am Penychain to Liverpool as far as Caernarvon and was awaiting the relief to the 9.15am Liverpool to Penychain that ran in two parts on this day, to attach on front as pilot. *W.G. Rear.*

Caernarvon. May 1947. The antecedents of the DMU was the push-pull working, or motor trains as the LMS called them. The propulsion unit was different but the principal was the same. Ex LNWR 0-6-2T No.**27603** of 7B (Bangor) shed pulls out of Caernarvon station Up and Down platform with the working to Bangor. Motor trains were seen daily at Caernarvon at this period in time, with two trips in succession between Bangor and Caernarvon in the middle of the day. The unit was normally on the Bethesda branch service but reduction of services on that line meant that the unit was available for a couple of hours. Eventually the locomotive was replaced by one of the new Ivatt 2-6-2T engines, which improved the lot of the traincrew, for the LNW engines were awkward engines to work, particularly for the fireman who had very cramped conditions in which to work. Indeed the only time he had sufficient space to move was when the driver was off the footplate! Notice the old station nameboard - yellow background with black painted wording. Behind in the Bangor bay the siding was filled with sheeted wagons awaiting transfer to the goods shed. *J.M. Dunn.*

Caernarvon. 12th November 1966. Stanier Class 5 4-6-0 No. **44875** of Llandudno Junction shed shunts the goods yard which seems devoid of stock, apart from the cattle trucks on the back road. These had been sent from Holyhead for cleaning and would then be held until required. There had been some track modifications by this time. The Afonwen line had closed and the Llanberis line had been lifted, the scissors crossover by No. 2. signal box had been stripped to a single point. The Up platform line had also been lifted but the goods line survived. No. 1. signal box had gone and all signalling and point movements were worked from No. 2. box. *A. Wyn Hobson.*

Caernarvon. January 1965. Fairburn 2-6-4T No. **42283** pulls out of the upper goods yard at Caernarvon with a freight for Menai Bridge yard. The engine was in excellent condition, and had been overhauled recently in Cowlairs Works. One LNER tradition incorporated whilst in the works was to paint the shed name 'BANGOR' on the front bufferbeam, and Bangor men took a pride in having this cleaned to perfection to declare their home shed to the world. To the left of the picture can be seen the water tower, a remnant from the days when Caernarvon had an engine shed, although the water tower remained in use, and in fact the loco had topped up its tanks before setting out for Menai Bridge. The locomotive is crossing the pointwork leading down to the coal yard, which was at harbour level. Above the tank wagon can be made out the fertiliser and livestock feed store and beyond that, the petrol storage tanks. At the time of the photograph, the tank farm was being enlarged, but the extra capacity did not benefit the railway, for the petrol was delivered from Ellesmere Port by coastal tanker. Today, all have all gone and the site stands ready for development. *E.N. Kneale*

Caernarvon. 6th October 1951. One of the more sedate turns at Bangor was the 'Caernarvon Shunt', which was in a link of two turns - early and late - which involved working Light Engine out and back to Bangor at the start and finish of each shift. A variety of motive power was used which was delegated to the older forms of motive power available which generally meant the surviving ex LNWR locomotives or one of the L.&Y. 0-6-0 tender engines that were coming to the end of their life and would not be unduly taxed by shunting duties. The work entailed remarshalling the two early morning freight trains from Mold Junction and then shunting wagons into and out of the goods shed and the coal yard. Various other freight workings spent time in the yard as part of the turn and these provided work for the shunting engine to do. Here No.**6899** in run down condition, heavily begrimed and leaking like a sieve stands on the back road of the goods yard near the site of the former locomotive shed awaiting the next move. The engine had not been renumbered and only the 'L.M.S.' lettering had been painted out. The LNWR CME's were never renowned for their consideration of the train crew and the fireman's lot was not a comfortable one, with extremely cramped working conditions adding to the discomfort.

D.H. Ballantine.

Caernarvon. July 1953. Eventually the LNWR engines were transferred away or sent for scrap, and most traincrews heaved a sigh of relief. The ex L.& Y. 0-6-0's took their place, but these also began to thin out, those remaining being required for the Port Siding or the Port Penrhyn trips or the Permanent Way Yard shunt. The spare engine allocated to the Caernarvon Shunt alternated between one of the Stanier Class 3 2-6-2T or an Ivatt Class 2 2-6-2T and either of these locomotives was a distinct improvement on what had gone before. No.**40129** is seen here in repose, which was a suitable duty for this type of engine, where the steaming demands were not great, and the cab was more commodious than before, it even had a passably comfortable seat! The two man link was regarded as 'Old Man's Duties' with drivers who were perhaps not in the best of health being allocated a spell. The fireman were also senior passed men who were waiting promotion to be marked up, and were available at short notice for driving duties. The 'Shunt' was a suitable duty with which to substitute a passed cleaner and in these cases he could learn some of the rudimentary elements of firing without causing his driver to have a heart attack! Indeed, the first turn the author worked as a passed cleaner was on the afternoon turn.

W.G. Rear.

Caernarvon. August 1953. As mentioned previously, various other locomotives called at the yard on freight workings, and part of their duty involved some shunting. Here Stanier 2-6-4T No.**42455** pauses on the Goods Line at Caernarvon on the return working from Llanberis. Train crew, shunter and goods clerk pose in front of the loco before resuming their tasks: the clerk back to his office, the train crew to couple up and make for home and the shunter to put the kettle on and have a brew! *W.G. Rear.*

Caernarvon. 17th May 1962. Stanier 2-6-4T No.**42489** of Bangor puts up a smokescreen as she pulls out of the Up platform with the 7.45am from Pwllheli to Bangor. This was the only steam worked passenger train of the day on the Afonwen branch at this time, the remaining passenger working being in the hands of the DMU's. The following month saw the introduction of the summer timetables and all of the DMU turns on the line reverted to steam. There was plenty of activity in the station goods yard and the sidings are full of wagons waiting to be placed in the coal yard or the goods shed or to be worked away.   *M.J. Mensing.*

Caernarvon. September 1962. Fairburn 2-6-4T No.**42676** rolls into Caernarvon with the 6.45pm from Llandudno Junction to Afonwen, the last Down working along the branch for the day. Notice the four arm bracket signal, which replaced the two three arm bracket signals seen in previous pictures. A raft of cattle trucks stand in the goods lines and on the coal yard sidings awaiting marshalling for the evening freight to Mold Junction. The footbridge over the tracks in the distance provided an excellent view of the station.   *E.N. Kneale.*

aernarvon. September 1952. Stanier 2-6-4T No.**42588** of Bangor shed pulls away from Caernarvon with the 3/50pm Afonwen to Bangor working. The leading van ries mails from Portmadoc. Behind the last coach can be seen No.1 Signal Cabin, built into the side of the embankment, which was reputed to be one of the draughtiest nal boxes in North Wales, and which unfortunately also housed some of the largest rats ever seen, in the interlocking room under the cabin. The loco is passing a three n bracket signal which controlled access to the Bangor Bay, the Up and Down platform and the Local platform respectively. This signal, and the three arm bracket nal alongside No.1 cabin were both replaced the following year by one four arm upper quadrant bracket signal. The lines in the foreground bearing right led down to coal yard and the density of traffic in the early 1950's necessitated using these lines to park wagons which would be incorporated into the evening freight to Mold ction. *W.G. Rear.*

Caernarvon. July 1964. An unidentified Stanier 2-6-4T pulls past the outer home signal with the 10.40am SO Penychain to Liverpool working. This had been piloted by another 2-6-4T that had been detached at Caernarvon, leaving the train engine to work on to Bangor where it would be replaced by a Class 5 4-6-0. The track had been recently reballasted, and gleams in the warm summer air. A yacht sits becalmed in the Menai Straits, visible over the roof of the leading carriage. As was usual with Penychain trains, every seat is taken, and passengers were standing in the guards van and the corridors. *W.G. Rear.*

Caernarvon. 10th April 1966. The lower goods yard at Caernarvon was rarely photographed. This view shows vans standing outside the fertiliser and livestock feed store, whilst mineral wagons are standing about the yard. Petrol tank wagons stand on the line that extended into the tank farm awaiting collection by the oil company. These wagons were propelled by a version of an industrial tractor, fitted with a large buffing plate on the front, with rubber pads affixed to lessen the impact. An old coach body stands on sleepers, and was at some time used as an office. In the upper yard some wagons stand on the coaling road alongside the water tank.   *A. Wyn Hobson.*

Caernarvon. 30th September 1970. Caernarvon station closed to all traffic on 5th January 1970, and contracts for demolition were advertised. However on 23rd May the Britannia Bridge over the Menai Straits caught fire and isolated lines on Anglesey from the mainland. It was decided to use Caernarvon station as a temporary Freightliner terminal and this came into use on 15th June 1970 and continued until 5th February 1972 when the totally rebuilt Britannia Bridge reopened to traffic. Apart from container traffic which was handled in the upper goods yard, other commodities were dealt with in the coal sidings. To deal with the shunting and movement of wagons, diesel shunter no.**12082** was based at Caernarvon for many months, travelling once a week to Bangor for refuelling. It was the last engine to be shedded at Caernarvon, and the first to be shedded since 1931. Here 12082 stands outside the fertiliser and livestock feed shed whilst wagons are offloaded into road tipper vehicles for onward carriage onto Anglesey.
    A.Wyn Hobson.

Caernarvon. 4th April 1967. One of the factors that saved the line from Bangor to Caernarvon was the quantity of freight that was handled in the town's goods yards. After the closure of the Afonwen line, this diminished, but there was still plenty of freight handled daily, which was covered by Llandudno Junction trip engine working. The B.R. Sultzer Class 24 No. **D5006** shunts the lower coal yard, removing empty tank wagons from the Esso tank farm which would be worked to Ellesmere Port. There plenty of activity in this yard, mostly coal traffic, although some vans can be seen outside the fertiliser and animal feed store. The upper yard is full of cattle wagons ght from Holyhead for cleaning and store. All that remained of the loco shed is the small outside office and the manhole in a stone pillar. *A. Wyn Hobson*

Caernarvon. 1952. Stanier 2-6-T No. **40132** of Bangor shed working the Caernarvon Shunt pulls out the lower (coal) yard. No. **44445** the Nantlle goods meanwhile shunts wagons in the Excursion Platform road beyond the signal box. The water tank opposite the signal box is all that remained of the locomotive shed yard. The three-arm signal in the foreground and a similar three arm signal beyond No.1 signalbox in the distance was replaced by a four-arm upper quadrant signal shortly after this view was taken. The spire of Christ Church dominates the skyline. *W.G. Rear.*

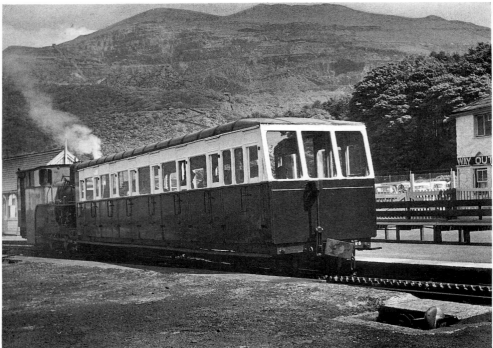

Llanberis Station. Snowdon Mountain Railway. May 1961. The Snowdon Mountain Railway, the only rack railway in the British Isles, commences its $4^5/_8$ mile ascent of the north-western slopes of Snowdon, the highest mountain in England and Wales at the small picturesque town of Llanberis, 353 feet above sea level, situated 7 miles south-east of Caernarvon. When the London & North Western Railway opened its branch to Llanberis Sir Richard Moon, the LNWR chairman expressed an interest in extending the line to the summit of the highest of the five peaks that, towering above Llanberis comprise the Eryri chain, the highest peak being Y Wyddfa, 3560 feet above sea level and the present terminus of the SMR. However, the first sod was cut on behalf of the Snowdon Mountain Tramroad & Hotel Co., on 15 December 1894 by Enid Assheton Smith, the daughter of a prominent landowner. Engine No.2 *Enid*, bore this lady's name and that of No.1 was derived from the initials of Mrs Laura Alice Duff Assheton Smith, e.g. *L.A.D.A.S.* this engine is no longer in existence. The line is laid to a gauge of 800mm (2 ft 7½ in) and Engine No.8 *Eryri* featured here, similarly to the line's other steam locomotives is a standard type of rack railway tank locomotive, built at Winterthur by the Swiss Locomotive & Machine Works, and came into service in 1923. Normal mountain railway procedure is followed in that the engine always travels to the summit chimney first, pushing the coach which is not coupled to the locomotive. The rack rail to Dr. Abt's system that will be engaged by the mechanism on No.8 observed between the running rails. *Norman Jones*

Y Wyddfa. The Summit. Snowdon Mountain Railway. May 1961. Engines No.**5** *Moel Siabod* Works No.989 of 1896 and No.**8** *Eryri* Works No.2870 of 1923, stand at the Summit, their drivers admiring the view across the valley, towards Llyn Cwellyn, Y Garn, 2080 ft, Mynydd Mawr 2290 ft. and the wonderland that is Snowdonia beneath their gaze. The climb to the summit is continuous from the outset, the easiest gradient of 1 in 50 being that encountered on the first 350 yards out of Llanberis station. Nor is the route straight, forty-two per cent is on curved track. Stations are situated at Hebron, where the gradient is 1 in 10, Halfway, with a gradient of 1 in 11, Clogwyn, where the gradient is 1 in 15 and the Summit where the gradient is 1 in 20. When our picture was taken in addition to the platforms there was a pleasant restaurant (left) with adequate toilet facilities, known as the Summit Hotel opened in 1936. It was of course necessary for all water and supplies for the 'hotel' to travel over the Snowdon Mountain Railway and the morning Workman's train carried a 700 gallon water tank in addition to food-stuffs and other necessaries. The railway does not operate during the months of winter, usually welcoming visitors from Easter to the end of the first week in October, although high winds or snowstorms may sometimes cause disruption to services.   *Norman Jones.*